UNDERSTANDING
the
HAGGADAH
and the
PASSOVER SEDER

COMMENTARIES-HALACHAH-HISTORY
MIDRASHIM-GEOGRAPHY-BIOGRAPHIES

by
Sol Scharfstein

KTAV PUBLISHING HOUSE, INC.

Copyright © 2001
KTAV Publishing House, Inc.
900 Jefferson Street
Hoboken, New Jersey 07030
Fax: 201-963-0102
Email: ktav@compuserve.com

**This book
is lovingly dedicated to
my wife
and my b'seder-mate
Edythe J.**

Acknowledgments

Numerous multitalented people have worked hard to bring *Understanding the Haggadah* to life. They believed in the project and labored long and arduously, critiquing and editing.

I wish to thank the following for their assistance. It is their sense, sensibility, scholarship and artistry that have shaped the text.

Robert Milch
Bernard Scharfstein
Herbert Stavsky
Oscar Rijo-designer

The final responsibility for any omissions, errors and mistakes are my own.

TABLE OF CONTENTS

INTRODUCTION

Jewish holidays and ceremonies are luminescent stars which add joy and substance to our journey through life. The rich, timeless rituals and traditions of the historic faith of Judaism are unbreakable links in the chain of tradition which stretches from Abraham and Sarah to everyone at the Seder table.

Just think, as Jews you can trace your family lineage to the seventy hungry souls, who because of drought reluctantly went to Egypt to live with their long-lost kinsman Joseph. The Pharaoh welcomed and settled them in Goshen, where they prospered. As has happened throughout Jewish history, first they were were welcomed and later reviled and enslaved.

Directed by a mysterious voice from the midst of a burning bush, Moses the Redeemer dared to confront the Pharaoh. After ten miraculous plagues the Hebrew slaves, with raw dough strapped to their kneading trays, made the Exodus from Egypt, the land of bondage.

As they made their escape, the Israelites, through a mystical experience at Mount Sinai, met Adonai. In the biblical account, historical and religious experience became entwined. The experience of the Exodus became a vehicle for religious instruction and the holiday of Passover was born.

Since that momentous event, wherever Jews have lived, even though few in number they have been a center of attraction, sadly, mostly as a tormented minority. Yet, miraculously the Jews have survived, as a people, as a religion, and as a force for justice and freedom. Jews in every generation have tasted the "bread of affliction"

as prisoners by the rivers of Babylon,
as gladiators in the Roman circuses,
as Marranos burned to death by the Inquisition,
as innocents raped and murdered by the Crusaders,
as victims of Russian and Polish pogroms,
as peaceful settlers murdered by Arab terrorists,
as refuseniks exiled to Siberia by the communist killers,
as the six million holy martyrs murdered by the Nazis in the Final Solution.

At the Seder, a young child innocently asks, "Why is this night different from all other nights?"

We answer, Because in each generation Jews have survived thousands of nights of servitude, hate, murder, and now we sit together as a family in freedom, friendship, warmth and joyfully participate in a freedom Seder.

The Seder is our victory celebration. We have survived!

The message of Passover is not only for Jews, but for all the world: to preserve, protect and extend the freedom of thought, expression and religion to all peoples.

ABOUT THE TEXT
The Hebrew text is traditional. The English translation, has in some cases been simplified so it can be read with increased ease and comprehension.
May you the reader, find in it the spiritual sustenance that has sustained the Jewish people throughout the generations.

THE
STORY
OF
PASSOVER

The Exodus

How does this night differ from all other nights? On all other nights we eat bread and matzah; why on this night do we eat only matzah?
We were slaves to Pharaoh in Egypt; and Moses was sent to free our people from bondage . . .

The question is the same every year, and so is the answer. For both are part of a ceremony that has remained unchanged for centuries upon centuries. This ceremony is called the *Seder*, and it marks the beginning of Passover.

What Is Passover?

Passover, or Pesach, is many things. It is a festival of freedom, when we recall how the Almighty released our ancestors from slavery in Egypt and helped a free people come into existence.

Passover is an agricultural festival, reminding us of the Land of Israel in ancient times. Our ancestors were farmers, and Passover marked the beginning of the grain harvest.

Passover is also a pilgrimage festival. Three times a year, the Israelites went in joyous procession to Jerusalem, to celebrate the festivals of Passover, Shavuot, and Sukkot.

Passover is all of these things, but it is especially a holiday for children. Our ancestors were instructed: "You shall tell it to your child." The Seder service, the reading of the Haggadah, the Four Questions, the stealing of the afikomen–all these are meant for boys and girls, to teach them the importance of this great holiday in the history of the Jewish people.

Turn Back the Clock

To learn the story of Pesach we must wend our way across the sands of time to a distant age and a strange land. There, in ancient Egypt, lived Joseph, the favorite and gifted son of Jacob. Joseph had been sold by his brothers to Midianite merchants, who in turn had brought him to Egypt.

One day Joseph was thrown into prison on false charges. Soon afterwards, Pharaoh, the ruler of Egypt, had a strange dream in which seven lean cows devoured seven fat ones. Not a single wise man or wizard in all the land could tell the meaning of the dream. Then Joseph, who had interpreted dreams for the royal cupbearer and the royal baker, was called before the Pharaoh.

"I have dreamed a dream and none can interpret it," said the Pharaoh. Joseph answered, "God is the interpreter of dreams. Perhaps through me He shall grant the Pharaoh peace of mind."

Joseph listened and then told the Pharaoh that his dream meant that seven years of famine would follow seven years of plenty in the land of Egypt.

Joseph Becomes Governor

The Pharaoh rewarded Joseph by making him governor over all the land. The new governor built huge granaries to be filled during the years of plenty. When the years of famine came, the full granaries saved Egypt from starvation.

Hyksos in Egypt

A time of famine came to Canaan, and the thoughts of the patriarch Jacob turned longingly to the fertile land of the Nile, where food was plentiful, even as other countries experienced famine. At Joseph's invitation, Jacob brought his family and flocks to Egypt.

The Pharaoh assigned the territory of Goshen to the Israelites. It was good grazing land, and for many years the Israelites lived there in peace.

Some historians believe that these events occurred around 1700 B.C.E., during the time when the Hyksos, a warlike tribe from Syria, swept into Egypt. The Hyksos ruled Egypt for about 120 years. Joseph was probably a high-ranking official under one of these powerful foreign rulers.

Slaves of the Pharaoh

Eventually the Hyksos were defeated, and Egyptian kings once more ruled over the land. The new Pharaohs, as the Bible tells us, "did not know Joseph." No longer were the Israelites respected as the privileged descendants of a noble ancestor. Instead they were enslaved. Some historians believe that this took place during the reign of Rameses II (ca. 1290-1224 B.C.E.). Egypt was a growing empire at this time, and the Pharaohs had great need for slaves to build new cities and magnificent palaces.

Rameses feared an uprising among the slaves and took cruel precautions to prevent it. He issued a decree that all male children born to the Israelites must be killed. In this merciless way, Rameses hoped to keep the Israelites from growing in numbers.

Baby Moses

Soon after this decree was issued, a male child was born to Jochebed, an Israelite woman, and her husband, Amram, of the tribe of Levi. To save the infant, they put him in a basket and set him afloat among the bulrushes of the Nile. The baby was found by an Egyptian princess while she and her handmaidens were bathing in the river.

The princess called the baby Moses, which means "drawn out of the water."

As a boy, Moses was given all the advantages enjoyed by members of Egypt's royal family.

Fighting for Freedom

One day Moses, now a prince, was outraged to see an Egyptian overseer beating an Israelite slave. Moses killed the Egyptian overseer and fled to the land of Midian in the Sinai desert. There he became a shepherd, living with a Kenite priest named Jethro. Moses married Jethro's daughter Zipporah, who bore him two sons.

The Burning Bush

In the rugged mountains of Sinai, Moses had an inspiring experience. Through a vision of a burning bush that was not consumed, God told him to go down to Egypt, confront Pharaoh, and lead the slaves to freedom. At first Moses refused, but eventually he accepted the responsibility. From that time forward, Moses was a man dedicated to the great task of leading his people to freedom.

Many obstacles were placed in his path by the Pharaoh. Again and again Moses, accompanied by his brother Aaron, stood before Pharaoh and pleaded for the Israelites. Pharaoh, full of power, turned a deaf ear to his pleas.

Ten Plagues

Egypt had to be stricken by ten disastrous plagues before Pharaoh, fearing the wrath of the God whom Moses and his people worshipped, finally consented to release the Israelites and allow them to leave the land. A multitude of about 600,000 men, in addition to women, and children left Egypt on that memorable night of the Exodus. There was barely time to prepare the food they would need.

The Israelites left so hurriedly that they had no time to bake their bread. They spread the raw unleavened dough on pieces of wood and tied them onto their shoulders. The hot desert sun baked the dough into matzot. This was the origin of the law of eating unleavened bread *(matzot)* on Passover, the festival that commemorates the victory won for freedom so many centuries ago.

The Exodus: A March to Freedom

So the great march out of Egypt began, with families gathered together, each with its own tribe, twelve tribes in all. However, Pharaoh suddenly changed his mind and sent charioteers to bring the slaves back. According to the Bible, Moses did not dare lead them by the established route, which was dangerously near Egypt's border forts, where soldiers might have attempted to prevent their escape. Instead, the great throng of people, young and old, carrying their meager belongings, marched slowly eastward to avoid the border posts.

The Sea of Reeds

The march was halted suddenly by an obstacle that seemed to be insurmountable. Silent and disheartened the Israelites stood, the light of hope slowly fading from their eyes as they gazed at the vast expanse of water before them. They had come to the end of dry land, to the shores of the Sea of Reeds (*Yam Suf*), the Suez arm of the Red Sea.

Those who looked back in the direction of their former homes were greeted by a sight that chilled their already sinking hearts. Bearing down upon them was a column of Egyptian soldiers. With the sea before them and the army of Pharaoh closing in from behind, the Israelites were trapped.

The Miracle

Then, miraculously, a strong east wind rose. It drove back the waters of the sea, making a path of dry land. With joyful hearts, the throng followed Moses to the opposite shore. In fierce pursuit, Pharaoh's soldiers also took the dry path through the Sea of Reeds, but the wind turned and the tide rolled in. Back rushed the waters, engulfing the chariots and drowning the soldiers.

Free at Last

The Bible tells of how the Israelites rejoiced when they found themselves safely across the sea. Moses composed a poem of praise to God. The women danced joyously to the music of their timbrels and sang a song composed by Miriam, Moses' sister. Ahead of them lay untold dangers, but on this great day there was but one song in the hearts of the Israelites, a song of gratitude for their newly won freedom.

The Long Trek

The Israelites wandered for 40 years until they reached Canaan, the Promised Land beyond the river Jordan. In Canaan they began a new life. They built homes and planted vineyards and celebrated their harvest festivals.

Since those days, we begin the celebration of Pesach on the eve of the 15th day of Nisan. During the week of the festival (observed for seven days by Reform Jews and Israelis, for eight by others) we eat unleavened bread to remind us of the bread our ancestors baked in haste when they left the land of Pharaoh.

The Exodus from Egypt

Archaeologists, historians, and Bible scholars have always been interested in learning more about the Exodus. They have been concerned with such questions as: Who was the Pharaoh of the Exodus? When did the Exodus take place? What route did the Israelites follow? and so on. They have found the answers to some of these questions.

On the basis of historical and archaeological evidence, most scholars believe that the Exodus took place around the begining of the 13th century B.C.E. (about 3,300 years ago), and that Rameses II was the Pharaoh of the Exodus. Here are some of the reasons they give:

1. The Bible tells us that the Hebrews lived in Goshen, near the Pharaoh's palace. This is in the Nile Delta in Egypt. Historians have learned that Rameses II built his capital in the Nile Delta.

2. The Bible tells us that the Hebrews built the store-cities of Pithom and Rameses for the Pharaoh. Archaeologists have found these cities. The city of Rameses was originally called Avaris, but it was rebuilt by Rameses II and renamed after him.

3. Archaeologists have excavated some of the ancient cities of Canaan. These excavations have shown that in the period several decades after 1290 B.C.E., many of the cities underwent much destruction, apparently from a war. This date is in keeping with the biblical account of the conquest of Canaan by the Children of Israel, which began under the leadership of Joshua after their 40 years of wandering in the desert.

PASSOVER IN TEMPLE TIMES

The Torah mandates: *"Three times each year, every male among you must appear before God."* The three times referred to were the holidays of Sukkot, Passover, and Shavuot, known in Hebrew as the *Shalosh Regalim*, or Three Pilgrimage Festivals.

According to the sages, everyone was required to appear before God except for women, minors, the infirm, and the aged. Even those who were not required to attend often participated in the pilgrimage. In practice, whole families made the pilgrimage together. Before Jerusalem became the capital, the pilgrimages were made to local shrines and to the Tabernacle in Shiloh.

The Pilgrims

Pilgrims were called *olei regel*, meaning "those who go up by foot." They were so called because Jerusalem is located high in the hills of Judea and the pilgrims had to climb by foot to reach the Temple. Ancient sources state that hundreds of thousands made their way to the Temple during each of the Shalosh Regalim.

The Talmud describes that Jews from as far as Babylon, Persia, Egypt, Ethiopia, Asia Minor, and Rome came to worship in the Temple on the Three Festivals.

The pilgrims traveled in large groups or caravans. They marched with flying banners announcing the name of their clan, town, or village. Many of the caravans were accompanied by musicians who played marching songs. Psalms 42, 82, and 122 are designated as Psalms of Ascent and were sung as the pilgrims ascended to Jerusalem.

Bikkurim

The object of the pilgrimage was to bring *bikkurim* (first fruits) and offer a sacrifice at the Temple. The Torah also commands: "None shall appear empty-handed. Every person shall give as they are able." The sages decided that the minimum offering was to be three pieces of silver. The proceeds were to be used for the upkeep of the Temple and to care for the sick, aged, and infirm.

The Temple in Jerusalem

The gates to the city were a maze of stalls and shops selling food, clothing, shoes, medicines, and imported goods from all over the ancient world. Farmers and shepherds wandered through the streets, amazed at the variety of goods, the babel of languages, and the hubbub of business transactions. Outside the gates it was carnival time, with storytellers, magicians, and acrobats to entertain the children. Inside the gates the atmosphere was dominated by the Temple and its religious rituals. At festival time, Jerusalem was a sea of color decorated with flowers and green branches. Crowds of pilgrims streamed toward the Holy Temple in the heart of the city. Silver trumpets sounded and choirs of Levites sang as the priests poured fresh spring water from golden pitchers onto the altar. The assemblage of thousands of voices joined the prayer "We pray, O Lord, save us and make us prosperous."

The Necessity for Pilgrimages

Pilgrimages were a cultural, political, and religious weapon in the battle for the survival of the Jewish state. The pilgrimage reunions helped mold the separate tribes into a single cultural, political, and military entity.

Israel was surrounded by idol-worshiping nations whose religious rituals during the harvest seasons were enticing to isolated Israelite farmers and shepherds. The pilgrimages to Jerusalem helped combat the pagan rites of the idol worshipers and kept the ancient Jewish traditions alive. They reinforced the faith and reaffirmed the covenant with God that was made at Mount Sinai. In the city squares, priests and Levites lectured the pilgrims on Jewish law and on the teachings of the Torah. Israelite farmers and shepherds lived dull, hard, lonely lives. They worked from early light to total darkness, raising their crops and tending their animals. The pilgrimages were also social occasions: a time for them to celebrate, a relief from the arduous daily regimen.

The Passover Pilgrimage

The pilgrimage of Passover, which starts on the 15th day of the month of Nisan, is also identified by two biblical names: *Chag Ha-Matzot* (Festival of Matzot) and *Chag Ha-Pesach* (Festival of the Paschal Lamb). Both names have historical significance. Chag Ha-Pesach reminds us of the events leading up to the Exodus, and Chag Ha-Matzot commemorates the events following the Exodus. In addition, Passover is also called *Chag Ha–Aviv* (Spring Holiday) because it marked the season of the new cereal crops in ancient Israel.

This agricultural theme is continued with the beginning of the *Omer*, or *Sefirah* ("counting"), which starts on the night of the second Seder and ends fifty days later on Shavuot.

The Season of Freedom

The Torah tells us that Passover is *Zeman Cheruteinu* (Season of Our Freedom). The Roman conquerors of Israel in the 1st century C.E. were very much aware of the Jewish thirst for freedom and were especially alert during the Passover pilgrimage. At Pesach time, when the city was crowded with pilgrims, Jerusalem became a hotbed of revolt. Roman spies searched the crowds for rebels. Agitators who were caught preaching rebellion were condemned to death by crucifixion.

The Passover Haggadah

The Passover Haggadah contains the story of five rabbis, Eliezer, Yehoshua, Elazar, Akiva, and Tarfon, who were at a Seder and spent the whole night discussing the story of the Exodus. Sometime later, Rabbi Akiba and Bar Kochba led such a revolt, and both lost their lives in the fight for freedom.

The Counting of the Omer

The time between Passover and Shavuot became a time of seriousness and prayer. The farmer prayed to God for a successful harvest and a year of plenty and gladness. Passover was the season of the barley harvest, and Shavuot was the season of the wheat harvest. On the day after Passover, the Temple priests would make a special sacrificial offering of a measure of grain, called an *omer*. The priest would mix the omer of grain with oil and frankincense and wave it up and down and from side to side. This ceremony was interpreted as a prayer for God to protect the harvest from strong winds and harsh weather.

Starting from this day, the people would count the days between the waving of the omer and Shavuot. We still call these seven weeks (or forty-nine days) the time of *Sefirat Ha-Omer,* which means "Counting of the Omer."

Both of these rituals, the wave offering and the bikkurim, were suspended after the destruction of the Temple, and a new historical motif, the giving of the Torah on Mount Sinai, was introduced as the focus of the Shavuot festival.

THE PASSOVER SEDER

Preparing for Passover

Preparations for the holiday begin in every home many weeks before Pesach. Everything in the house is scrubbed and polished. Carpets are cleaned, floors are scrubbed, fresh curtains are hung. Just before Passover, year-round kitchen utensils are put away, to be replaced by those specially reserved for the holiday.

Then comes the matzah, enough to last for the entire festival period. Matzah is the only kind of bread permitted in a Jewish home on Passover.

Matzah Designs

In the time of the Talmud, the perforated matzot were quite artistic. In the house of Rabbi Gamliel, the little holes in the matzot made figures: animals, flowers, and such. The perforating was done with a tool that looked like a comb. In later years, the perforating tool was a wheel; it had sharp teeth and a handle. The perforator would run the wheel through the matzot at right angles in rows about one inch apart.

In olden times, matzot were made in the home as well as by professional bakers. During the Middle Ages, there were community ovens. The matzot were usually made in a round shape, but sometimes they were triangular.

Ma'ot Chittim

A fund known as *Ma'ot Chittim* ("wheat money") was set up in every community. This was to provide Passover provisions for the poor and the needy. In our day, we can participate in the mitzvah of tzedakah by contributing to the Ma'ot Chittim fund.

A Special Matzah

A special kind of matzah is called *shemurah matzah* ("guarded matzah"). Many Orthodox Jews use it, particularly on the two Seder nights.
Shemurah matzah is made from wheat that is watched from the time of harvesting, milling, and baking. The wheat is carefully protected against leavening, either by rain swelling the grain or dampening the flour, or by too much kneading and slow baking.

Around 1875, matzah-baking machinery was invented in England. Soon after, it was introduced in America. Although some matzot are still made by hand, most Passover matzot today are made by machine. Actually, matzot are used all year round. On Passover, however, only matzot which are prepared for the holiday may be eaten. The only day one may not eat matzot is the day before Pesach; this is to ensure that they are eaten with greater enjoyment during the Seder.

Selling the *Chametz*
Since traditionally there must not be any *chametz* or leavened bread in Jewish homes on Passover, Orthodox Jews perform a ceremony known as *mechirat chametz* several days before the holiday. A bill of sale is written out, and all the chametz is "sold" to a non-Jew for the duration of Passover. This transaction is usually handled as a collective sale by the rabbi of the congregation, but in order for it to be valid, the members must personally ask the rabbi to be their agent. The bill of sale is prepared with the understanding that the chametz will be returned immediately after the holiday.

The Search for *Chametz*
The last cleansing ceremony, *bedikat chametz*, takes place on the night before the first Seder night. To symbolize the change from the old to the new, from leavened to unleavened bread, a family member takes ten bits of bread and put them on window sills and shelves. Now, someone else takes a quill and a wooden spoon, and with the help of children, looks for chametz.

Naturally, someone finds the bits of bread. The bread is brushed onto the wooden spoon. When all the bread crumbs are found, they are wrapped, together with the spoon, in a piece of cloth and put away until morning. Then they are burned, together with any bread left from breakfast.

After ten in the morning on the day before Passover (*erev* Pesach) no chametz should be eaten. Neither are matzot eaten that day, so that the real Pesach matzot will taste fresh and new when they are eaten at the Seder. Everything has been taken care of. The holiday is about to be ushered in. For eight days, beginning at sundown on the 15th day of the month of Nisan, the family celebrates the festival of Pesach. The first two and the last two days are traditionally observed as full holidays by Orthodox and Conservative Jews; the intervening four days (*Chol Ha-Mo'ed*) are semi-holidays.

The Seder

On the first Seder night the table is decked in gleaming white, the candles cast a warm, flickering glow, and the proud wine cups stand ready to play their part in the annual drama of the Pesach Seder. A properly prepared Seder table is an important part of the Passover celebration.

The Hebrew word Seder means "order" or "arrangement"; and the arrangement of foods at the Seder tells of the many-sided meaning of Passover, the great festival that marks the birth of a free people thousands of years ago and still has an important message for every one of us.

What items can be found on the Seder table?

Candles

As on every Sabbath and festival, candles grace the table. The blessing over the candles gives warmth to their light as they cast a holiday glow over the Seder and those who have come to celebrate Passover.

The Haggadah

"You shall tell it to your child," says the Torah. The Haggadah (from the Hebrew *hagged*, "to tell") recounts the Passover story and adds thanksgiving prayers and children's songs. It makes Pesach a holiday the whole family looks forward to.

Four Cups of Wine

Everyone at the Seder table drinks four cups of wine in the order mentioned in the Haggadah. There are four cups because in the Torah, God's promise to free the Israelites from slavery is repeated four times.

The Cup of Elijah

At the Seder, each person drinks four cups of wine. But a fifth cup of wine is also poured. Known as the *Kos Eliyahu*, it honors the prophet Elijah. The Bible tells us that Elijah did many wonderful and miraculous deeds. There are many legends about Elijah and the wonderful things he could do. According to one of the legends, Elijah will come back to earth. When he does, it will be the beginning of a golden age. The whole world will be at peace and we will all love one another and be good to one another.

The fifth cup of wine at the Seder is for Elijah. It symbolizes our hope that Elijah will soon come and that everyone in the world will learn to live in peace.

The Matzah Cover

In the center of the Seder table is a decorated cloth with three pockets in which we place three whole matzot. Each of the matzot represents one of the three classes of ancient Israelites: priests (*kohanim*), Levites (*levi'im*), and lay people (*yisraelim*).

Half of the middle matzah will be used as the *afikomen*, or dessert. The child who hides the afikomen will receive a gift for returning it. The Seder cannot be completed until the afikomen is returned.

Many families now add a fourth matzah which is called the Matzah of Hope. This fourth matzah helps us to remember that there are still Jews who live in countries where they cannot celebrate Passover in freedom.

K'arah

Next to the matzah cover is the *K'arah*, or Seder plate. On it are *maror* (bitter herbs), a shankbone, *charoset* (a mixture of apples, nuts, and wine), a roasted egg, and *karpas* (a green vegetable, such as parsley or celery). Each of these stands for something important.

Roasted Egg

The egg symbolizes the festival offering *(Korban Hagigah)* sacrificed on Pesach in the Temple of Jerusalem. The egg is used in the Seder because it is a Jewish symbol of mourning, in this case for the destruction of our ancient Temple where the sacrifices were brought.

Maror

The bitter herbs (usually horseradish) are for the bitterness of slavery. It was bitter in Egypt in those days; it is no less bitter for people wherever there is tyranny.

Karpas

Greens (lettuce, parsley, or celery) symbolize the poor nourishment the Israelites had while in Egyptian slavery. The dipping of karpas into saltwater is to remind us of the salty tears they wept under Egypt's cruel yoke.

Matzah

After the ten plagues, the Israelites, pressed by the Egyptians to leave, snatched up their bread dough even though it had not yet risen. This is memorialized by the unleavened matzah. There are three special matzot at the Seder. Half of the middle matzah will be used as the afikomen, or dessert. For children who find the afikomen, there usually is a present for returning it upon request.

Shankbone

This roasted bone is a symbol of the Pesach lamb sacrificed at the Temple of our ancestors.

Charoset

Although this mixture of apples, nuts, cinnamon, and wine symbolizes the mortar made by our ancestors under the lash of Egyptian taskmasters, it tastes delicious. Why? Because its sweetness, it is said, is a symbol of God's kindness which made even slavery bearable.

The Haggadah

The Haggadah has already been mentioned, but it deserves closer attention, for it plays a central role at the Seder.

The Haggadah is a kind of guidebook for the celebration of Pesach. It has directions on how to conduct the Seder, explanations of the Pesach symbols, selections from Psalms (113–118), interesting stories, children's folk songs, riddles, and prayers. Most important of all, it tells the story of why we celebrate Passover.

The Haggadah has a long history. It is more than 2,000 years old. Even before it was written down, the leader of the family would tell the story of Pesach at the Seder table. He was following the commandment in the Bible, "You shall tell your child in that day, saying: 'It is because of that which the Lord did for me when I came forth out of Egypt.' " The very term Haggadah comes from the Hebrew word *hagged*, which means "to tell."

As time went by, more parts were added to the Haggadah, even though it was still not written down: prayers, hymns, selections from the Mishnah. By the Middle Ages so much had been added that it was necessary to put the Haggadah in writing. But even then the Haggadah was not a separate book, but a part of the prayerbook. Soon after the Middle Ages the Haggadah became a book in its own right.

What the Haggadah Tells

It is in the Haggadah that we learn how the sacrificial lamb (pesach), unleavened bread (matzah), and bitter herbs (maror) were used in ancient times. It includes the beautiful thanksgiving psalms of Hallel, and ends with the songs Adir Hu and Chad Gadya.

One of the most stirring parts of the Haggadah is recited at the beginning of the Seder, beginning with *Ha-Lachma Anya*, "This is the bread of affliction." The leader lifts the plate of matzah, and recites,

This is the bread of affliction which our ancestors ate in the land of Egypt. Let all who are hungry come and eat. Let all who are in need come and celebrate Pesach with us. Now we are here. Next year may we be in the Land of Israel. Now we are slaves. Next year may we be free people.

Ha-Lachma Anya is one of the oldest parts of the Haggadah. It is written in Aramaic, a language spoken by our ancestors in Israel almost 2,000 years ago. It was once customary for the head of the house to step out into the street and recite Ha Lachma Anya, so as to invite any poor people to the Seder. Today the invitation to the poor is recited inside the home, but the spirit of hospitality remains the same.

The Four Questions

Following Ha-Lachma Anya, the youngest child recites the Four Questions:
Why is this night different from all other nights?
1. On all other nights, we eat either leavened or unleavened bread. Why on this night do we eat only unleavened bread?
2. On all other nights, we eat all kinds of vegetables and herbs. Why on this night do we eat only bitter herbs?
3. On all other nights, we do not dip even once. Why on this night do we dip twice?
4. On all other nights, we eat sitting upright or reclining. Why on this night do we all recline?

The Four Children

Then comes the long story of the Exodus from Egypt, followed by descriptions of the four different kinds of children a family might have: wise, contrary simple, and one who asks no questions.

The wise child eagerly asks about Pesach and why it is celebrated, and is given a full explanation.

The contrary child scoffs at Pesach, and would have been unworthy of being saved in the time of the Exodus from Egypt.

The simple child asks a simple question and gets a simple answer.

The fourth child asks nothing, but the parents volunteer the information. This child, too, is told why we celebrate Pesach.

The Haggadah and Art

The Haggadah has played an important part in the development of Jewish art. In Haggadot, artists found many subjects they could illustrate: the four children, the ten plagues, Jacob's ladder, the crossing of the Red Sea, the matriarchs and patriarchs, the baking of matzah, and many other things. The artists of the Haggadah all expressed themselves in their own way.

The Amsterdam Haggadah

In the 17th century, Amsterdam, Holland, became a center of Jewish printing. In 1695, the famous Amsterdam Haggadah appeared "in the house and to the order" of Moses Wesel. This Haggadah was illustrated with copper engravings. On the title page are the words: "Formerly the pictures used to be cut in wood. That was not so beautiful. Now that they are engraved in copper, everyone will realize the difference, which is like that between light and dark." In a later Amsterdam Haggadah more pictures were added, borrowed from a woodcut Haggadah which had been published in Venice, Italy.

The Darmstadt Haggadah

Even rarer than the few surviving early printed Haggadot are the manuscript Haggadot from a still earlier era before the invention of printing. These handwritten and painstakingly illustrated Seder guides, each of them a work of art, are one-of-a-kind items. Outstanding among them is the world-famous Darmstadt Haggadah.

The Darmstadt Haggadah was written on parchment in the 14th century by Israel ben Meir of Heidelberg. Israel only did the lettering. One artist then painted in large gold-and-blue initials and decorated the borders; a second artist drew scenes of Jewish life, especially Seder scenes. Mingled among the Seder scenes are illustrations of wildlife. Birds, bears, lions, and other animals abound on the pages.

Many Heidelberg Jews had come from France. In the Haggadah, they wear the lavish holiday dress of prosperous French citizens. The beautiful Darmstadt Haggadah belonged for centuries to German Jewish families. In 1780, a Baron Hopsch bought it for his collection. It then made its way into the library of Darmstadt, Germany, where it has remained to this day.

The Seder Is Ended

The Seder is ended, the Haggadot are closed. The questions have been answered and the story has been told.

The Samaritan Passover

The Samaritans were once a fairly sizable religious community. Today only about 600 people still accept the Samaritan faith. Half of them live in the town of Nablus, near Mount Gerizim. The other half live in Holon near Tel Aviv.

In ancient times the Samaritans were often in conflict with the Jews. They acknowledge Moses as a prophet and claim to be descended from Ephraim and Manasseh, the two sons of Joseph. They accept the Torah and the Book of Joshua as holy, but not the rest of the Bible.

Passover is the Samaritans' most important holiday. It is celebrated on top of Mount Gerizim. The Passover feast is celebrated just as it was thousands of years ago. A lamb is sacrificed and matzot are baked the ancient way.

Faraway Customs

Customs vary, but the Seder is observed wherever there are Jews, and the Haggadah is the guidebook.

The Caucasian Jews of southern Russia have an interesting ritual. They greet the Passover seated on the earth, dressed in their best clothes, with a spear close at hand. This is their way of portraying the dangers that beset the Israelites in the hurried Exodus from Egypt.

And in the eastern provinces of Portugal, near the Spanish border, in several communities descended from the Marranos, there is a custom that shows what life was like in the days of the Inquisition. Since the entire family would have been killed if the Inquisition's police had found a single matzah in their homes, these people do not have a Seder at home. Instead they go to the countryside for a festive outing. It may look like a picnic to outsiders, but the Marrano participants make sure to say a special prayer in memory of the Seder service their ancestors enjoyed.

Now We Are Free

After the festive meal, which has been eaten very slowly, to symbolize that we are now a free people and no longer slaves who can be forced to hurry, traditional songs are sung by the whole family.

The family sings: *"Who knows one? I know one! One is our God in heaven and on earth. . . . Who knows two? I know two,"* and so on, up to thirteen, which is the number of the qualities of God.

The Little Kid
Then comes the final song for which the children have been waiting all evening. It is about a little goat that father bought for two coins. The song seems to have an endless number of verses, but at last it comes to a stop with:

> *Then came God*
> *Who smote the Angel of Death,*
> *Who slew the slaughterer,*
> *Who killed the ox,*
> *Who drank the water,*
> *That quenched the fire,*
> *That burned the stick,*
> *That beat the dog,*
> *That bit the cat,*
> *That ate the little goat*
> *That father bought with two coins.*

Ani Ma'amin
In some homes a new ceremony has been introduced before the door is opened for the prophet Elijah. During the ceremony we remember the six million Jews who were murdered by the Nazis, and the heroes of the ghetto revolts.

We sing the song *Ani Ma'amin*. This song of hope was sung by the martyrs in the concentration camps.

The words were written in accordance with the teachings of the famous Jewish philosopher Moses Maimonides.

> *I believe*
> *I believe, I believe*
> *with all my faith, with all my faith*
> *that the Messiah will come,*
> *that the Messiah will come*
> *I believe.*

That is the story of Pesach, a heroic revolt against oppression and glorious freedom from slavery. Throughout the ages, Passover has symbolized freedom: whether escape from Egypt, rescue from the Crusaders of the Middle Ages, or liberation from the Nazis.

Just as we overcame our enemies in the land of Egypt, so will the Jewish people ever vanquish its oppressors. That is the message of Passover which must forever be kept alive in our hearts.

הַגָּדָה שֶׁל פֶּסַח

THE
PASSOVER
HAGGADAH

THE SEARCH FOR CHAMETZ

On the evening before the first Seder (if the first Seder falls on Saturday night, this is done on the preceding Thursday evening), after the evening service, the head of the household makes the final preparation for Passover by searching for leaven throughout the house. It is customary to place ten pieces of bread in various places, so that when the search is made, leaven is found. Otherwise, the benediction recited before the ceremony would be in vain.

Before the ceremony of searching for leaven begins, a candle or flashlight is lit with which to conduct the search, and the following prayer is recited:

1 בָּרוּךְ אַתה יְיָ אֱלֹהֵינוּ מֶלֶךְ הָעוֹלָם, אֲשֶׁר קִדְּשָׁנוּ בְּמִצְוֹתָיו

2 וְצִוָּנוּ עַל בִּעוּר חָמֵץ:

The search for leaven is conducted. After the leaven has been gathered and wrapped securely, the following is said:

3 כָּל־חֲמִירָא וַחֲמִיעָא, דְּאִכָּא בִרְשׁוּתִי, דְּלָא חֲמִתֵּה, וּדְלָא

4 בְעַרְתֵּהּ, וּדְלָא יְדַעְנָא לֵהּ, לִבָּטֵל וְלֶהֱוֵי הֶפְקֵר, כְּעַפְרָא

5 דְאַרְעָא:

On the morning after the search, at about ten o'clock, all the leaven that has remained in the house, together with all collected during the search the previous evening, is burned. If the first Seder falls on Saturday night, the burning takes place on Friday, before noon, and bread (challah) may still be eaten until Sabbath morning. At the burning of the leaven (or on disposal after an early Sabbath meal when the first Seder falls that evening) the following is recited:

6 כָּל־חֲמִירָא וַחֲמִיעָא, דְּאִכָּא בִרְשׁוּתִי, (דַּחֲזִתֵּהּ וּדְלָא חֲזִתֵּהּ,)

7 דַּחֲמִתֵּהּ וּדְלָא חֲמִתֵּהּ, דְּבִעַרְתֵּהּ וּדְלָא בִעַרְתֵּהּ, לִבָּטֵל

8 וְלֶהֱוֵי הֶפְקֵר, כְּעַפְרָא דְאַרְעָא:

Leaven The evil inclination, *yetzer harah,* is called the leaven in the dough. Just as leaven causes dough to ferment and rise, so does the *yetzer harah* cause a person's evil inclination to awaken and rise to the surface.

Chametz Fermented or leavened wheat, rye, oats, and barley are called *chametz.* When these grains come in contact with water, the process of leavening will begin within 18 minutes. In the case of hard or salted water, leavening will take place instantly. Flour is produced from grain that has been washed and tempered. Tempering is a process by which grain is softened by soaking in water. Tempered flour and all products made with it are therefore chametz.

THE SEARCH FOR LEAVEN

*On the evening before the first Seder (if the first Seder falls on
Saturday night, this is done on the preceding Thursday evening), after
the evening service, the head of the household makes the final preparation for Passover by searching for leaven throughout the house. It is customary to place ten pieces of bread in various places, so that when the
search is made, leaven is found. Otherwise, the benediction recited
before the ceremony would be in vain.*

*Before the ceremony of searching for leaven begins, a candle or flash-
light is lit with which to conduct the search, and the following prayer is
recited:*

Blessed are You, Eternal our God, Ruler of the universe,
 Who made us holy with commandments, and
 commanded us to remove the <u>leaven.</u>

*The search for leaven is conducted. After the leaven has been gathered
and wrapped securely, the following is said:*

Any leaven that may still be in the house, which I have notseen
 or have not removed, shall be as if it does not exist, and as the
 dust of the earth.

*On the morning after the search, at about ten o'clock, all the leaven that has
remained in the house, together with all collected during the search the previous
evening, is burned. If the first Seder falls on Saturday night, the burning takes
place on Friday, before noon, and bread (challah) may still be eaten until
Sabbath morning. At the burning of the leaven (or on disposal after an early
Sabbath meal when the first Seder falls that evening) the following is
recited:*

Any leaven that may still be in my possession, which I have or
 have not seen, which I have or have not removed, shall be as if
 it does not exist, and as ownerless as the dust of the earth.

Leaven. The sources for restricting leaven on Passover are found in the
Torah: "You shall eat matzot for seven days, but on the first day you shall
destroy all leaven from your homes, for whoever eats leaven from the first
day to the seventh day, that soul shall be cut off from Israel" (Exodus.12:19).

THE MIXING OF FOODS

When Passover falls on Thursday and Friday, in order that it may be permissible to cook on the festival for the Sabbath (one is only permitted to cook on a holiday for that day alone), the head of the household must perform the ritual of Eruv Tavshilin (mixing of foods) before the festival, indicating that the preparation for the Sabbath was begun before the festival, and thus it may be continued on the festival itself. This is done by taking some food for the Sabbath (matzah and cooked fish, meat, or a boiled egg), putting these on a plate, raising it, and reciting the following prayer.

1 בָּרוּךְ אַתָּה יְיָ אֱלֹהֵינוּ מֶלֶךְ הָעוֹלָם, אֲשֶׁר קִדְּשָׁנוּ בְּמִצְוֹתָיו
2 וְצִוָּנוּ עַל־מִצְוַת עֵרוּב:

Blessed are You, Eternal our God, Ruler of the universe,
Who made us holy with commandments, and
commanded us to observe the Eruv.

3 בַּהֲדֵין עֵרוּבָא יְהֵא שָׁרֵא לָנָא לְמֵיפָא, וּלְבַשָּׁלָא, וּלְאַצְלָיָא,
4 וּלְאַטְמָנָא, וּלְאַדְלָקָא שְׁרָגָא, וּלְתַקָּנָא, וּלְמֶעְבַּד כָּל־
5 צָרְכָּנָא, מִיּוֹמָא טָבָא לְשַׁבַּתָּא. לָנוּ, וּלְכָל־יִשְׂרָאֵל, הַדָּרִים
6 בָּעִיר הַזֹּאת:

With this Eruv it shall be permissible for us to bake, cook, keep food warm, light the candles, and make all necessary preparations on the festival for the Sabbath. This shall be permitted for us and for all Jews who live in this city.

Eruv Tavshilin. An *eruv tavshilin* is a halachic device which allows one to cook food on the festival for use on the Shabbat that follows immediately afterward. In order to cook on the festival for use on Shabbat, one must prepare an *eruv tavshilin* which serves as a reminder that the cooking done on the festival is for Shabbat only. This eruv consists of a matzah and something cooked, such as a boiled egg or a piece of fish, and is prepared before the start of the festival. It symbolically serves as the beginning of the preparation of food for Shabbat. Any subsequent cooking done on the festival is considered to be a continuation of the preparation before the festival.

LIGHTING THE PASSOVER CANDLES
On the Sabbath, add words in parentheses

1 בָּרוּךְ אַתָּה יְיָ אֱלֹהֵינוּ מֶלֶךְ הָעוֹלָם, אֲשֶׁר קִדְּשָׁנוּ בְּמִצְוֹתָיו,

2 וְצִוָּנוּ לְהַדְלִיק נֵר שֶׁל (on Sabbath: שַׁבָּת וְ)יוֹם טוֹב:

Blessed are You, Eternal our God, Ruler of the universe.
Who sanctified us with commandments, and commanded us
to light (the Sabbath and) the festival lights.
*Baruch atah adonay elohey-nu melech ha-o-lam asher
kid-sha-nu b'mits-vo-tav v'tsiva-nu l'had-lik ner shel
Shabbat ve-shel yom tov.*

3 בָּרוּךְ אַתָּה יְיָ אֱלֹהֵינוּ מֶלֶךְ הָעוֹלָם, שֶׁהֶחֱיָנוּ, וְקִיְּמָנוּ,

4 וְהִגִּיעָנוּ, לַזְּמַן הַזֶּה:

Blessed are You, Eternal our God, Ruler of the universe.
Who has kept us in life, and sustained us, and enabled us
to reach this festive season.
*Baruch atah adonay elohey-nu melech ha-o-lam
sh'heh-chi-ya-nu v'ki-ya-ma-nu v'hi-gi-ya-nu la-z'mahn ha-zeh.*

To light the festival lights Passover starts with the lighting and blessing of the holiday candles. Why do we light candles on Passover? Because, just as Creation began with the happy words "Let there be light," so does the Sabbath and every Jewish holiday and Sabbath begin with light.
We welcome Passover by performing the mitzvah of lighting the holiday candles. The brightly burning candles create an atmosphere of love, peace, and family harmony.

THE SEDER TABLE

At the Seder table you will find the following items

THE KITTEL

It is customary for the Seder leader to wear a white gown (kittel) in honor of Passover. The white color is a symbol of freedom.
White also reminds us of the priests (Kohanim) in the Holy Temple who dressed in white robes.

THE HAGGADAH

The Men of the Great Assembly, during the Second Temple period, established a fixed text for the Haggadah that included the various blessings, prayers, the Four Questions, and other elements of the Seder ritual. Over the course of time, additions were made to the basic text from various midrashic sources. The sages called this text the Haggadah, "meaning that which is told," based on the Torah's commandment to tell your child the story of the Exodus.
Despite minor changes and the addition of a number of songs at the end of the Seder, the basic text of the Haggadah is the same as the one written by the Men of the Great Assembly.

FOUR CUPS OF WINE

The four cups of wine are associated with specific mitzvot at the Passover table. The first cup belongs to step 1 in the Seder: Kadesh. The second cup is associated with step 5, Maggid, the retelling of the Passover story. The third cup is joined to the twelfth step, Barech, the grace after the meal. The fourth and final cup comes at the end of the Hallel.

ELIJAH'S CUP

At the Seder table a special goblet is filled with wine for Elijah the prophet in the symbolic hope that he will bring health and prosperity to the celebrants. In religious literature Elijah is believed to appear and come to the aid of Jewish communities that are in distress.
During circumcision ceremonies a symbolic seat called the Chair of Elijah is set aside for his coming and his blessing. In Europe, chairs specially made for Elijah are to be found in many synagogues. The Cup of Elijah is sometime identified as the fifth cup. It symbolizes the fifth Torah expression of freedom: "and I will bring you out." (Exodus 6:8). This expression refers to the ingathering of the exiles into the Holy Land. This promise was partly validated in 1948 with the establishment of the State of Israel.

THE SEDER PLATE

An important feature of the Seder table is the Seder plate. In Hebrew the Seder plate is called *K'arah*. Each symbol has a special place on the Seder plate. These are the five symbols:

1. Charoset is a mixture of chopped apples, nuts, and raisins mixed with cinnamon and wine.
The appearance of the Charoset reminds us of the cement the Israelites made when they were slaves in Egypt.
2. Karpas is parsley or any green vegetable, The karpas reminds us of the trees, vegetables, and flowers that come to life each spring.
3. Maror is bitter herbs. They remind us of the bitter lives of the Israelites in Egypt.
4. Z'roa is a roasted shankbone. The z'roa reminds us of the Pascal sacrifice the Israelites brought to the Holy Temple in Jerusalem on Passover.
5. Baytzah is a roasted egg. It is a symbol of life. It also represent the festival offering (*Korban Hagigah)* brought to the temple on Passover.

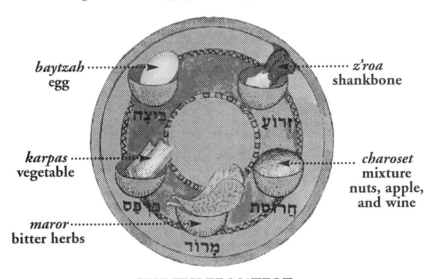

baytzah egg · · · · · · · · · · · · · · · *z'roa* shankbone

karpas vegetable · · · · · · · · · · · · · · · *charoset* mixture nuts, apple, and wine

maror bitter herbs · · · · · · · · · · · · · · ·

THE THREE MATZOT

The three matzot in the matzah bag are said to represent the three classes of Israelites: Kohen (priest), Levi (Levite), and Yisroel (Israelite). During the Seder each of the three matzot is used to perform a mitzvah. The top matzah, the Kohen, is used during the Motzi Matzah benediction. The middle matzah is broken in half; one half is wrapped in a napkin and becomes the afikomen. The third, the Israelite matzah, is used during the Korech ceremony In this ceremony we eat the bitter herb and matzah together and recite a Haggadah selection.

THE ORDER OF THE SEDER

The following fourteen Seder symbols are your guide to the Seder service:

1. You say Kiddush over the wine.
Kadesh קַדֵּשׁ

2. You wash your hands.
Urhatz וּרְחַץ

3. You eat a green vegetable dipped in salt water.
Karpas כַּרְפַּס

4. The leader divides the middle matzah and hides part of it for the afikomen.
Yachatz יַחַץ

5. You recite the Haggadah and tell the story of Israel and Egypt.
Maggid מַגִּיד

6. You wash your hands and say the blessings.
Rachtzah רָחְצָה

7. You say two blessings over the matzah.
Motzi-Matzah מוֹצִיא מַצָּה

8. You recite a blessing over the bitter herbs
Maror מָרוֹר

9. You eat a sandwich of matzah and maror.
Korech כּוֹרֵךְ

10. You enjoy your Seder meal. שֻׁלְחָן עוֹרֵךְ
Shulchan Orech

11. You find and eat a piece of the Afikomen.
Tzafun צָפוּן

12. You say the grace after the meal.
Barech בָּרֵךְ

13. You recite the Hallel.
Hallel הַלֵּל

14. End of Seder. You sing songs of freedom.
Nirtzah נִרְצָה

THE ORDER OF THE SEDER

The basic structure of the Seder was set about 2,000 years ago in the time of the Mishnah. The Seder is a happy celebration with a procession of 14 scenes or steps. The rabbis wanted us to remember the steps, so they composed a lilting rhyme with 14 key words. We start the Seder with a splash of song and sing this rhyme.

THE ORDER OF THE SEDER

The following fourteen Seder symbols are your guide to the Seder service:

1 קַדֵּשׁ.

2 וּרְחַץ.

3 כַּרְפַּס.

4 יַחַץ.

5 מַגִּיד.

6 רָחְצָה.

7 מוֹצִיא

8 מַצָּה.

9 כּוֹרֵךְ.

10 שֻׁלְחָן עוֹרֵךְ.

11 צָפוּן.

12 בָּרֵךְ.

13 הַלֵּל.

14 נִרְצָה.

RECITATION OF THE KIDDUSH (1) קַדֵּשׁ
Everyone at the table has a cup of wine
THE FIRST CUP

If the holiday begins on Friday night, start here
and add the words in parentheses.

1 וַיְהִי־עֶרֶב וַיְהִי־בֹקֶר

2 **יוֹם הַשִּׁשִּׁי:** וַיְכֻלּוּ הַשָּׁמַיִם וְהָאָרֶץ וְכָל־צְבָאָם: וַיְכַל

3 אֱלֹהִים בַּיּוֹם הַשְּׁבִיעִי, מְלַאכְתּוֹ אֲשֶׁר עָשָׂה, וַיִּשְׁבֹּת

4 בַּיּוֹם הַשְּׁבִיעִי, מִכָּל־מְלַאכְתּוֹ אֲשֶׁר עָשָׂה: וַיְבָרֶךְ אֱלֹהִים

5 אֶת־יוֹם הַשְּׁבִיעִי, וַיְקַדֵּשׁ אֹתוֹ, כִּי בוֹ שָׁבַת מִכָּל־מְלַאכְתּוֹ,

6 אֲשֶׁר־בָּרָא אֱלֹהִים לַעֲשׂוֹת:

The first cup The brightly burning candles have sanctified the Seder. The table is set in "order." Family, friends, relatives, and guests are seated around the table. The Haggadot are opened. The first ceremony is known as Kadesh. Why do we recite the Kiddush on Passover? Because when we recite the Kiddush, we are thanking God for making such a wonderful and beautiful world.

KADESH - RECITATION OF THE KIDDUSH (1)
Everyone at the table has a cup of wine
THE FIRST CUP
If the holiday begins on Friday night, start here and add the words in parentheses.

It was evening and morning on the sixth day.
The heavens and the earth and all that was within them had
been completed. The Eternal finished all the work of
creation by the seventh day. And the Eternal rested on
the <u>seventh day</u> from doing the work of creation. And
the Eternal blessed the seventh day and made it holy,
because on it the Eternal had rested from all the work of
creation.

The seventh day is one of God's greatest gifts to humankind. Shabbat
goes back to the creation of the world. God created the world in six days,
and rested on the seventh day. Even in Egypt, under slave conditions, the
Israelites observed the Sabbath.

Our sages tell us that Moses was filled with sorrow when he saw his people
working so hard. He went to Pharaoh and said: "Let your slaves rest
every seventh day. Then they will have renewed strength and will work
even harder the other six days." The Pharaoh listened to his advice. Thus,
even when they were slaves in Egypt, the Hebrews celebrated Shabbat.

If Passover begins on a weekday, start here.

1 בָּרוּךְ אַתָּה יְיָ אֱלֹהֵינוּ מֶלֶךְ הָעוֹלָם, בּוֹרֵא, פְּרִי הַגָּפֶן:

2 בָּרוּךְ אַתָּה יְיָ אֱלֹהֵינוּ מֶלֶךְ הָעוֹלָם, אֲשֶׁר בָּחַר בָּנוּ

3 מִכָּל־עָם, וְרוֹמְמָנוּ מִכָּל־לָשׁוֹן, וְקִדְּשָׁנוּ בְּמִצְוֹתָיו, וַתִּתֶּן

4 לָנוּ יְיָ אֱלֹהֵינוּ בְּאַהֲבָה on Sabbath שַׁבָּתוֹת לִמְנוּחָה וּ)

5 מוֹעֲדִים לְשִׂמְחָה, חַגִּים וּזְמַנִּים לְשָׂשׂוֹן, אֶת־יוֹם (on

6 Sabbath; הַשַּׁבָּת הַזֶּה, וְאֶת־יוֹם) חַג הַמַּצּוֹת הַזֶּה. זְמַן

7 חֵרוּתֵנוּ, (on Sabbath; בְּאַהֲבָה) מִקְרָא קֹדֶשׁ, זֵכֶר לִיצִיאַת

8 מִצְרָיִם. כִּי בָנוּ בָחַרְתָּ, וְאוֹתָנוּ קִדַּשְׁתָּ, מִכָּל־הָעַמִּים.

9 בְּאַהֲבָה (on Sabbath; וְשַׁבָּת) וּמוֹעֲדֵי קָדְשֶׁךָ (on Sabbath;

10 וּבְרָצוֹן) בְּשִׂמְחָה וּבְשָׂשׂוֹן הִנְחַלְתָּנוּ: בָּרוּךְ אַתָּה יְיָ, מְקַדֵּשׁ

11 (on Sabbath הַשַּׁבָּת וְ)יִשְׂרָאֵל וְהַזְּמַנִּים:

Recite Shehecheyanu on page 38.

This day of Passover Passover is the most celebrated and festive of our holidays. It begins on the eve of the 15th day of the Hebrew month of Nisan and lasts for eight days. On Passover we remember how Moses freed the Israelites, who were slaves in Egypt. The holiday received its name from the Hebrew word *pesach*. When all the firstborn sons of the Egyptians were killed in the tenth plague, the Angel of Death passed over (*pasach*) the homes of the Jews and their lives were saved. Passover is also called the Feast of Matzot, because the Jews left Egypt in such a hurry they did not have the time to let the dough for bread rise. This flat, hard. unleavened bread is called matzah. Another name for Passover is the Season of our Freedom, because at this time of year the Israelites left the slavery of Egypt. Human beings should not have to serve another person against their will. It is true that the Jews had slaves in Bible times, but our rabbis explain that these were really servants. According to Jewish law, Hebrew servants could serve their master no longer than six years, and were rewarded handsomely upon leaving.

The fruit of the vine The four cups of wine also represent the four nations that enslaved Israel and from which they were redeemed: Egypt, Babylonia, Persia and Greece, and for those who drink the fifth cup, Rome.

If Passover begins on a weekday, start here;
Blessed is the Eternal our God, ruler of the world
  who created *<u>the fruit of the vine.</u>*

> Baruch atah adonay elohey-nu melech ha-o-lam borey-p'ree
> ha-ga-fen.

Blessed is the Eternal our God, ruler of the world, who has
  chosen us from among all peoples and raised us from
  among all other peoples and made us holy with divine
  commandments and in love, gave us (Sabbaths of rest and)
  festivals for joy, seasons and holidays for happiness, among
  them (this Sabbath and) <u>this day of Passover,</u> the season of
  our freedom, a day of sacred assembly commemorating the
  Exodus from Egypt. <u>You have chosen us,</u> sanctifying us
  among all peoples by granting us (the Sabbath and) your
  sacred festivals (lovingly and) in joy and happiness. The
  Eternal who sanctifies (the Sabbath and) the people of
  Israel and the festival seasons.

Recite Shehecheyanu on page 38.

You have chosen us. For 2,000 years the phrase "You have chosen us"
has been a powerful weapon used by anti-Semites to imply that Jews
believe that they are better, wiser and more deserving than other nations
of the world.
The covenant by which Israel was chosen was never meant to be one of
superiority; it is a call for greater responsibility and a demand that they
promote the welfare of all mankind. Jews believe that the Eternal is the
God of all creation and does not "choose" and does not make distinctions
between nations and people.

This day of Passover Passover has four separate names which describe
  four different events in Jewish history.
1. Passover is the Festival of Freedom.
2. Passover is also the Holiday of the Paschal Lamb because on that fateful
night, all the firstborn Egyptians died, but the Jewish homes were saved
because their doorposts was smeared with the blood of the paschal lamb.
3. Finally, Passover is the Festival of Matzot. Passover is historically and
religiously all of these, but for us it is also a time of family togetherness
when generations unite and celebrate as one family.

If the festival falls on Saturday night add the following:

1 בָּרוּךְ אַתָּה יְיָ אֱלֹהֵינוּ מֶלֶךְ הָעוֹלָם, בּוֹרֵא מְאוֹרֵי הָאֵשׁ:

2 בָּרוּךְ אַתָּה יְיָ אֱלֹהֵינוּ מֶלֶךְ הָעוֹלָם, הַמַּבְדִּיל בֵּין קֹדֶשׁ

3 לְחוֹל, בֵּין אוֹר לְחֹשֶׁךְ, בֵּין יִשְׂרָאֵל לָעַמִּים, בֵּין יוֹם

4 הַשְּׁבִיעִי לְשֵׁשֶׁת יְמֵי הַמַּעֲשֶׂה. בֵּין קְדֻשַּׁת שַׁבָּת לִקְדֻשַּׁת

5 יוֹם טוֹב הִבְדַּלְתָּ. וְאֶת־יוֹם הַשְּׁבִיעִי מִשֵּׁשֶׁת יְמֵי הַמַּעֲשֶׂה

6 קִדַּשְׁתָּ. הִבְדַּלְתָּ וְקִדַּשְׁתָּ אֶת־עַמְּךָ יִשְׂרָאֵל בִּקְדֻשָּׁתֶךָ:

7 בָּרוּךְ אַתָּה יְיָ, הַמַּבְדִּיל בֵּין־קֹדֶשׁ לְקֹדֶשׁ:

8 בָּרוּךְ אַתָּה יְיָ אֱלֹהֵינוּ מֶלֶךְ הָעוֹלָם, שֶׁהֶחֱיָנוּ, וְקִיְּמָנוּ,

9 וְהִגִּיעָנוּ, לַזְּמַן הַזֶּה:

Reclining on the left side, drink the first cup of wine.

HAVDALAH

If the festival falls on Saturday night add the following:
Blessed is the Eternal our God, Ruler of the universe,
Creator of light and fire.

Blessed is the Eternal our God, Ruler of the world, Who
has let us see the difference between the holy and the
plain, between light and darkness, between Israel and the
other nations, between the seventh day and the six days
of Creation. You have made a difference between the
holiness of the Sabbath and the holiness of the Festivals,
and You have made the seventh day holier than the six
days of work. You have set and made holy Your people
Israel with Your holiness.

Blessed are You, who makes a distinction between
holiness and holiness.

Blessed is the Eternal our God, Ruler of the universe, Who
has given us life and sustenance and brought us safely to
this happy season.

Baruch atah adonay elohey-nu melech ha-o-lam
sh'heh-chi-ya-nu v'ki-ya-ma-nu v'hi-gi-ya-nu la-z'mahn ha-zeh.

Reclining on the left side, drink the first cup of wine.

WASH THE HANDS (2) וּרְחַץ
Wash your hands, but do not say the blessing.

EAT A GREEN VEGETABLE (3) כַּרְפַּס
The leader of the Seder takes some parsley, or any other vegetable, and dips it into the salt water.
Everyone at the table says the following before it is eaten.

1 בָּרוּךְ אַתָּה יְיָ אֱלֹהֵינוּ מֶלֶךְ הָעוֹלָם, בּוֹרֵא, פְּרִי הָאֲדָמָה:

BREAK THE MIDDLE MATZAH (4) יַחַץ
The leader of the Seder breaks the middle matzah, leaving half in the matzah holder. The leader then hides the other half until after the meal, as the afikomen. In some homes, it is the custom to "kidnap" the afikomen and hold it for ranson. The child who returns the afikomen is usually rewarded with a small gift.

Washing the hands A religious ritual lifts a biological act from the realm of the physical and raises it to a spiritual level.

Karpas The karpas is a vegetable such as parsley, celery, lettuce or potatoes. At the Seder the karpas is dipped in salt water and eaten after the recitation of a blessing. The holiday of Passover is also known as Hag Ha-Aviv, the Spring Festival. The karpas reminds us of our ancestors who lived in the ancient land of Israel. Passover was a happy time and marked the beginning of the barley harvest.

URHATZ - WASH THE HANDS (2)
Wash your hands, but do not say the blessing.
KARPAS - EAT A GREEN VEGETABLE (3)
The leader of the Seder takes some parsley, or any other vegetable, and dips it into the salt water.
Everyone at the table says the following before it is eaten.
Blessed is the Eternal our God, Ruler of the universe, Creator of the fruit of the earth.

Baruch atah adonay elohey-nu melech ha-o-lam borey-p'ree ha-a-da-ma

YACHATZ - BREAK THE MIDDLE MATZAH (4)
The leader of the Seder breaks the middle matzah, leaving half in the matzah holder. The leader then hides the other half until after the meal, as the afikomen. In some homes, it is the custom to "kidnap" the afikomen and hold it for ranson. The child who returns the afikomen is usually rewarded with a small gift.

Yachatz The fourth ceremony of the Seder is Yachatz, the breaking of the middle matzah. Near the K'arah is a special matzah holder. The matzah holder has three matzot. Some say that the three matzot are for the three kinds of Jews that have existed since the days of the Bible: Kohen, the priest, Levi, the Levite, and Yisrael, the Israelite The leader breaks the middle matzah. One half is replaced into the matzah holder. The other half is wrapped in a napkin and becomes the afikomen. The word afikomen is Greek, and means "dessert." The afikomen is eaten at the end of the meal as a dessert. At this point in the Seder the leader hides the afikomen. The Seder cannot be completed without it. Returning the afikomen is a happy time. The child who returns the afikomen to the leader, so that the Seder can be continued, gets a special gift.

מַגִּיד THE PASSOVER STORY (5)

Uncover the Matzah. The recital of the Passover story begins with the following words:

1 הָא לַחְמָא עַנְיָא,

2 דִּי אֲכָלוּ אַבְהָתֶנָא בְּאַרְעָא דְמִצְרָיִם.

3 כָּל־דִּכְפִין יֵיתֵי וְיֵכוֹל,

4 כָּל־דִּצְרִיךְ יֵיתֵי וְיִפְסַח.

5 הָשַׁתָּא הָכָא,

6 לְשָׁנָה הַבָּאָה בְּאַרְעָא דְיִשְׂרָאֵל.

7 הָשַׁתָּא עַבְדֵי,

8 לְשָׁנָה הַבָּאָה בְּנֵי חוֹרִין:

This is the bread of bitterness This prayer was written about 1,600 years ago in Babylon, where many thousands of Jews lived. In this prayer we thank God for all the blessings we enjoy. We also invite people less fortunate than us to join us at the Seder.

The Ha Lachma Anya prayer talks about *lechem oni*, the poor person's bread. Matzah is *lechem oni* because it is pale and white like a poor person who has had very little to eat and works hard from morning till night. Like the poor person's bread, it is made only with flour, without nourishing ingredients like eggs and milk. And, like the poor person's bread, it is hard to eat and digest.

Let all who are hungry come and eat. There are two types of hunger; physical and psychological. Physical hunger can be cured by food. However, psychological hunger can be suffered by both rich and poor. Today the technological marvels of the 21st century have separated friends and families. Children, grandparents, parents, and relatives are spread across 3,000 miles of space and connected by wires, e-mail, and the Internet. Families have a hunger which cannot be satisfied by voice mail. The Seder releases us from our servitude and brings families, relatives, and friends together to satisfy their hunger for love and friendship.

MAGGID - THE PASSOVER STORY (5)
Uncover the Matzah.
The recital of the Passover story
begins with the following words:

This is the matzah of bitterness
Which our ancestors ate in the Land of Egypt.
Let all who are hungry come and eat.
Let all who are needy come
And celebrate the Seder with us.
Now we are here,
Next year may we be in the land of Israel.
This year we are like slaves,
Next year may we be free people.

Let all who are hungry come and eat. When we recite the Ha Lachma Anya we remind ourselves there are still many people who are poor and enslaved. We recite the Ha Lachma Anya at the Seder because Passover is known as the Festival of Freedom. On Passover we celebrate our freedom from slavery.

Let all who are hungry come and eat. The custom of inviting all who are hungry to come and eat originated in Babylonia. Therefore, the invitation is extended in Aramaic, the basic language spoken by the Jewish people who lived there. Today, a special fund called *Ma'ot Chittim*, meaning "Funds for Passover," distributes money so that the poor can enjoy their own Seder without degrading themselves by begging. Passover is not the only holiday which provides funds for the less fortunate. On all religious holidays, Jews participate in the mitzvah of helping the poor and underprivileged.

THE FOUR QUESTIONS
Cover the matzah and fill the second cup of wine.
The youngest child that is able, now asks the Four Questions.

1 מַה נִּשְׁתַּנָּה הַלַּיְלָה הַזֶּה, מִכָּל־הַלֵּילוֹת?

2 שֶׁבְּכָל הַלֵּילוֹת, אָנוּ אוֹכְלִין חָמֵץ וּמַצָּה, הַלַּיְלָה הַזֶּה

3 כֻּלּוֹ מַצָּה:

4 שֶׁבְּכָל הַלֵּילוֹת אָנוּ אוֹכְלִין שְׁאָר יְרָקוֹת, הַלַּיְלָה הַזֶּה

5 מָרוֹר:

6 שֶׁבְּכָל הַלֵּילוֹת אֵין אָנוּ מַטְבִּילִין, אֲפִלּוּ פַּעַם אֶחָת,

7 הַלַּיְלָה הַזֶּה שְׁתֵּי פְעָמִים:

8 שֶׁבְּכָל הַלֵּילוֹת, אָנוּ אוֹכְלִין, בֵּין יוֹשְׁבִין, וּבֵין מְסֻבִּין,

9 הַלַּיְלָה הַזֶּה כֻּלָּנוּ מְסֻבִּין:

Why four questions? There are four questions in the Haggadah because the word "child" is mentioned four times in the Torah in regard to the obligation of retelling the story of the Exodus.

The Torah states:

1. And it will be when your children shall say to you, What is the purpose of this ceremony. (Exodus 12:26).

2. And you shall explain to the child on this day, saying, Because of what God did for me when I left Egypt (Exodus 13:8).

3. And it shall be when your child asks you in the future, saying, What is this. (Exodus 13:14).

4. When at some time your child asks you, What is the meaning of these symbols and statutes. (Deuteronomy 6:20).

The Four Questions The Men of the Great Assembly (ca. 145 B.C.E.), who edited the basic text of the Haggadah, were well aware of the wheel of history. They produced a religious, historical. and literary masterpiece that has withstood the erosion of time and has been applicable to Jews in every circumstance and place. Each generation, on the basis of its own political and life experience, comes face to face with its own reality. At the Seder the children ask the Four Questions and the adults provide the historical answers.

THE FOUR QUESTIONS
Cover the matzah and fill the second cup of wine.
The youngest child that is able,
now asks the Four Questions.

Why is this night different from all other nights?
1. On all other nights we eat leavened bread or matzah.
   On this night . . .WHY only matzah.

2. On all other nights we eat all kinds of herbs.
   On this night. . . WHY only bitter herbs.

3. On all other nights we do not dip even one time.
   On this night . . . WHY do we dip twice.

4. On all other nights we eat either sitting or leaning.
   On this night . . . WHY do we sit in a leaning position.

Mah Nishtanah The Seder ceremony is a time for telling the Passover story and for Torah study and discussion. The learning session starts with the youngest child asking the Four Questions.

We sit in a leaning position In ancient times free people ate their meals in a leaning position or stretched out on couches. The leader conducts the Seder in a leaning position to show that we are all now *benai chorin*, a free people. All participants can, if they wish eat in a leaning posicion.

THE ANSWER

The leader uncovers the matzah and begins to answer.

1 עֲבָדִים הָיִינוּ לְפַרְעֹה בְּמִצְרָיִם, וַיּוֹצִיאֵנוּ יְיָ אֱלֹהֵינוּ מִשָּׁם,

2 בְּיָד חֲזָקָה וּבִזְרוֹעַ נְטוּיָה, וְאִלּוּ לֹא הוֹצִיא, הַקָּדוֹשׁ בָּרוּךְ

3 הוּא, אֶת־אֲבוֹתֵינוּ מִמִּצְרַיִם, הֲרֵי אָנוּ, וּבָנֵינוּ וּבְנֵי בָנֵינוּ,

4 מְשֻׁעְבָּדִים הָיִינוּ לְפַרְעֹה בְּמִצְרָיִם, וַאֲפִלּוּ כֻּלָּנוּ חֲכָמִים,

5 כֻּלָּנוּ נְבוֹנִים, כֻּלָּנוּ זְקֵנִים, כֻּלָּנוּ יוֹדְעִים אֶת־הַתּוֹרָה,

6 מִצְוָה עָלֵינוּ לְסַפֵּר בִּיצִיאַת מִצְרָיִם. וְכָל־הַמַּרְבֶּה לְסַפֵּר

7 בִּיצִיאַת מִצְרָיִם הֲרֵי זֶה מְשֻׁבָּח:

8 מַעֲשֶׂה בְּרַבִּי אֱלִיעֶזֶר, וְרַבִּי יְהוֹשֻׁעַ, וְרַבִּי אֶלְעָזָר בֶּן־עֲזַרְיָה,

9 וְרַבִּי עֲקִיבָא, וְרַבִּי טַרְפוֹן, שֶׁהָיוּ מְסֻבִּין בִּבְנֵי־בְרַק, וְהָיוּ

10 מְסַפְּרִים בִּיצִיאַת מִצְרָיִם, כָּל־אוֹתוֹ הַלַּיְלָה, עַד שֶׁבָּאוּ

11 תַלְמִידֵיהֶם וְאָמְרוּ לָהֶם: רַבּוֹתֵינוּ, הִגִּיעַ זְמַן קְרִיאַת

12 שְׁמַע, שֶׁל שַׁחֲרִית:

13 אָמַר רַבִּי אֶלְעָזָר בֶּן־עֲזַרְיָה. הֲרֵי אֲנִי כְּבֶן שִׁבְעִים שָׁנָה,

14 וְלֹא זָכִיתִי, שֶׁתֵּאָמֵר יְצִיאַת מִצְרַיִם בַּלֵּילוֹת. עַד שֶׁדְּרָשָׁהּ

15 בֶּן זוֹמָא. שֶׁנֶּאֱמַר: לְמַעַן תִּזְכֹּר, אֶת־יוֹם צֵאתְךָ מֵאֶרֶץ

16 מִצְרַיִם, כֹּל יְמֵי חַיֶּיךָ. יְמֵי חַיֶּיךָ הַיָּמִים. כֹּל יְמֵי חַיֶּיךָ

17 הַלֵּילוֹת. וַחֲכָמִים אוֹמְרִים: יְמֵי חַיֶּיךָ הָעוֹלָם הַזֶּה. כֹּל יְמֵי

18 חַיֶּיךָ לְהָבִיא לִימוֹת הַמָּשִׁיחַ:

Mitzrayim Egypt is an ancient country whose recorded history goes back about 6,000 years. From the beginning, it has been linked with Jewish history. The patriarchs Abraham and Jacob visited Egypt; Joseph was the vizier of Egypt; and Jewish history begins with the Exodus from slavery in Egypt.

King Solomon, in the 10th century B.C.E., married an Egyptian princess and made a treaty with Egypt. The prophet Jeremiah founded Jewish colonies in Egypt. A document discovered by archaeologists describes a Jewish colony of professional soldiers in Elephantine, an island in the Nile, in the 5th century B.C.E. *continued on page 47*

THE ANSWER

The leader uncovers the matzah and begins to answer.

Years ago, we were slaves to Pharaoh in <u>Egypt.</u> And the Eternal freed us from slavery "with a strong hand." Now, if the Eternal had not freed the Jews, then all of us today would still be slaves. Even if all of us were very wise, people of great intelligence, even if all of us were great Torah scholars, it would still be our duty to retell the story of our departure from Egypt. The more we talk about the story of freedom, the more we understand and appreciate the Eternal's miracle.

A story is told of Rabbi Eliezer, Rabbi Yehoshua, Rabbi Elazar ben Azariah, Rabbi Akiva and Rabbi Tarfon, who talked <u>all through the night</u> about the miracle of the Children of Israel leaving Egypt. The rabbis lost track of time so that their students had to interrupt them and remind them, "Rabbis, Rabbis, it is time to say the morning prayers."

Rabbi Elazar the son of Azariah said, "Here I am a man of 70 years old but I still do not understand why the story of the departure from Egypt should be told at night." Ben Zoma explained it. The Torah commands us saying: That you may remember the day of your leaving Egypt "all the days of your life." Ben Zoma explained, "The days of your life might mean only daytime; all the days of your life also includes the nights." The other sages explained it this way: "The days of your life refers to this world only, but all the days of your life includes also the time of the Messiah."

After Alexander the Great conquered Egypt in 333 B.C.E, many Jewish immigrants settled there. Jews continued to live in Egypt throughout the centuries. Sometimes conditions were favorable, but other times they were discriminated against. In the Middle Ages, the great scholar Maimonides was the doctor to Sultan Saladin. Egypt is a neighbor of the State of Israel. It was the first Arab country to make peace with Israel.

All through the night The Jews left Egypt during daytime on the 15th day of the Hebrew month of Nisan. The first half of the night was spent preparing for Passover, and the second half was spent preparing to leave. Egypt. By staying awake all night as the Israelites did, the rabbis placed themselves as if they too were leaving Egypt.

1 בָּרוּךְ הַמָּקוֹם. בָּרוּךְ הוּא. בָּרוּךְ שֶׁנָּתַן תּוֹרָה לְעַמּוֹ יִשְׂרָאֵל.

2 בָּרוּךְ הוּא. כְּנֶגֶד אַרְבָּעָה בָנִים דִּבְּרָה תוֹרָה. אֶחָד חָכָם,

3 וְאֶחָד רָשָׁע, וְאֶחָד תָּם, וְאֶחָד שֶׁאֵינוֹ יוֹדֵעַ לִשְׁאוֹל:

4 **חָכָם מָה הוּא אוֹמֵר** מָה הָעֵדֹת וְהַחֻקִּים וְהַמִּשְׁפָּטִים,

5 אֲשֶׁר צִוָּה יְיָ אֱלֹהֵינוּ אֶתְכֶם וְאַף אַתָּה אֱמָר־לוֹ כְּהִלְכוֹת

6 הַפֶּסַח: אֵין מַפְטִירִין אַחַר הַפֶּסַח אֲפִיקוֹמָן:

7 **רָשָׁע מָה הוּא אוֹמֵר** מָה הָעֲבֹדָה הַזֹּאת לָכֶם וְלֹא

8 לוֹ. וּלְפִי שֶׁהוֹצִיא אֶת־עַצְמוֹ מִן הַכְּלָל, כָּפַר בְּעִקָּר. וְאַף

9 אַתָּה הַקְהֵה אֶת־שִׁנָּיו, וֶאֱמָר־לוֹ: בַּעֲבוּר זֶה, עָשָׂה יְיָ לִי,

10 בְּצֵאתִי מִמִּצְרָיִם. לִי וְלֹא־לוֹ. אִלּוּ הָיָה שָׁם, לֹא הָיָה

11 נִגְאָל:

12 **תָּם מָה הוּא אוֹמֵר** מַה זֹּאת וְאָמַרְתָּ אֵלָיו: בְּחֹזֶק יָד

13 הוֹצִיאָנוּ יְיָ מִמִּצְרַיִם מִבֵּית עֲבָדִים:

14 **וְשֶׁאֵינוֹ יוֹדֵעַ לִשְׁאוֹל**, אַתְּ פְּתַח לוֹ. שֶׁנֶּאֱמַר: וְהִגַּדְתָּ לְבִנְךָ,

15 בַּיּוֹם הַהוּא לֵאמֹר: בַּעֲבוּר זֶה עָשָׂה יְיָ לִי, בְּצֵאתִי

16 מִמִּצְרָיִם:

Blessed is the Place. "Place" is a rabbinic term for God. The whole world is God's Place which He created. We also recite "Blessed is the Place" because we are blessing the place of family togetherness where, friends, relatives, and guests are seated at the Seder table and enjoying each other's

Blessed is the Place, who gave the Torah to Israel.
The Torah speaks about <u>four children</u>: one who is wise
and one who is contrary, one who is simple and one
who does not even know how to ask a question.

The wise child asks: "What is the meaning of the
rules, laws, and customs which the Eternal has commanded
us?" Explain to the **chacham** all the laws of
Passover from the start of the Seder until the afikomen.

The contrary child asks: "Why do you have a Seder?"
Notice that the rasha child says "you" but does not
include himself as a part of the Seder. Explain to the
rasha that we celebrate Passover because the
Eternal brought him out of Egypt.

The simple child asks: "What is a Seder?"
Explain to the child and say: "With a strong hand the
Eternal freed us all from Egypt."

To the one who does not even know how to ask
say: "We celebrate Passover because the Eternal saved us from
slavery in Egypt."

Four children These passages refer to four different types of Jewish
people with different attitudes and qualities. The rabbis give us this
self-examination text.

The Chacham, the wise person, is a member of a synagogue and is
involved in Jewish communal affairs and organizations. The wise one
wants to continue learning about Jewish customs, history, and law.

The Rasha, the contrary one, does not want to be a part of the Jewish
community and rejects his or her heritage. He does not actively
participate in the Seder.

The Tam, the simple person, admits, "I don't know anything about my
heritage, my Jewish education was neglected, but I am willing and ready
to learn."

The She'eno Yode'a Lishol, the person who does not even know enough
to ask but sees the other three, is in a dilemma: "Whom do I ask?" What
would you suggest to this person?

1 יָכוֹל מֵראשׁ חֹדֶשׁ, תַּלְמוּד לוֹמַר בַּיּוֹם הַהוּא. אִי בַּיּוֹם

2 הַהוּא, יָכוֹל מִבְּעוֹד יוֹם. תַּלְמוּד לוֹמַר, בַּעֲבוּר זֶה. בַּעֲבוּר

3 זֶה לֹא אָמַרְתִּי אֶלָּא בְּשָׁעָה שֶׁיֵּשׁ מַצָּה וּמָרוֹר, מֻנָּחִים

4 לְפָנֶיךָ:

5 **מִתְּחִלָּה עוֹבְדֵי כוֹכָבִים הָיוּ אֲבוֹתֵינוּ.** וְעַכְשָׁו קֵרְבָנוּ הַמָּקוֹם

6 לַעֲבוֹדָתוֹ. שֶׁנֶּאֱמַר: וַיֹּאמֶר יְהוֹשֻׁעַ אֶל־כָּל־הָעָם. כֹּה אָמַר

7 יְיָ אֱלֹהֵי יִשְׂרָאֵל, בְּעֵבֶר הַנָּהָר יָשְׁבוּ אֲבוֹתֵיכֶם מֵעוֹלָם,

8 תֶּרַח אֲבִי אַבְרָהָם וַאֲבִי נָחוֹר. וַיַּעַבְדוּ אֱלֹהִים אֲחֵרִים:

9 וָאֶקַּח אֶת־אֲבִיכֶם אֶת־אַבְרָהָם מֵעֵבֶר הַנָּהָר, וָאוֹלֵךְ אוֹתוֹ

10 בְּכָל־אֶרֶץ כְּנָעַן. וָאַרְבֶּה אֶת־זַרְעוֹ, וָאֶתֶּן־לוֹ אֶת־יִצְחָק:

11 וָאֶתֵּן לְיִצְחָק אֶת־יַעֲקֹב וְאֶת־עֵשָׂו. וָאֶתֵּן לְעֵשָׂו אֶת־הַר

12 שֵׂעִיר, לָרֶשֶׁת אוֹתוֹ. וְיַעֲקֹב וּבָנָיו יָרְדוּ מִצְרָיִם:

Worshipped idols. Terach, the father of Abraham, was an idol maker and he also prayed to them. The Midrash tells us that one day, as Abraham was watching his father sell an idol, a funny thought came to him: "It is silly for people to pray to a god chiseled and formed by my father's hands. It would make more sense for them to pray to my father, who after all, creates the idols. My father is more creative and therefore more godly than his stone and wooden idols." Abraham repeated this thought to his father. Terach laughed and considered it a great joke, but still continued to make and worship idols.

Worshipped idols. In Egypt the Israelites were redeemed from two types of bondage: physical bondage as slaves to Pharaoh, and spiritual bondage. At the Seder we remember and offer thanks for our physical and spiritual freedom. The Haggadah states: "At first our ancestors were idol worshippers." This phrase refers to Joshua's warning to the Israelites against idol worship, prior to his death.

Beyond the river The Hebrew word *Ivri,* meaning "Hebrew," is said to come from the word *ever,* meaning "beyond" or "on the other side." The sages say that Abraham the Hebrew, who believed in the One God, stood on the other side from the entire world of idol worshippers.

One might think that you should begin to tell the story of Passover from the new moon. The Torah, therefore, tells us "on that day." Saying "on that day," one might suppose that the Seder should start in the daytime. But, since the Torah adds "because of this," we learn that the ceremony does not begin until the time the matzah and the maror are set before you on Passover night.

At first our ancestors <u>worshipped idols</u>. Now, the Eternal is our God, and we worship the Lord. The Torah tells us: "And Joshua said to all the people: Adonai, God of Israel, said: In days of old your ancestors, that is Terach, the father of Abraham and Nahor, lived <u>beyond the river</u> (meaning Jordan). They worshipped idols. Then I took Abraham, your father, from beyond the river. I led them through the whole land of Canaan. Then I blessed his family by giving him a son, Isaac. And I gave Isaac two sons, <u>Jacob and Esau.</u> I gave Esau <u>Mount Seir,</u> but Jacob and his sons went down to Egypt."

Jacob and Esau. The relationship of Jews and Arabs is reflected in the Torah. It tells us that Abraham fathered Ishmael by Sarah's maid Hagar, and Sarah gave birth to Isaac.
Ishmael was the ancestor of the Arabs, so they see themselves as descended from Abraham. Since the Jews are descended from Abraham through Isaac, this makes the Jews and Arabs relatives.
Biologists have provided genetic confirmation that Arabs and Jews are descended from a common ancestral Middle East population some 4,000 years ago. This analytic technique is based on the Y chromosome, which passes unchanged from father to son.

Mount Seir The region of Mount Seir (later called Edom) was occupied by the descendants of Esau, the brother of Jacob. Edom was a mountainous country about 100 miles long. The summit of Mount Seir rises about 350 feet above the Araveh. In the days of the Hebrew monarchy the capital was called Sela. Sometime later the place was named Petra. Today, Petra is in the kingdom of Jordan.

1 בָּרוּךְ שׁוֹמֵר הַבְטָחָתוֹ לְיִשְׂרָאֵל. בָּרוּךְ הוּא. שֶׁהַקָּדוֹשׁ

2 בָּרוּךְ הוּא חִשַּׁב אֶת־הַקֵּץ לַעֲשׂוֹת, כְּמָה שֶׁאָמַר לְאַבְרָהָם

3 אָבִינוּ בִּבְרִית בֵּין הַבְּתָרִים. שֶׁנֶּאֱמַר: וַיֹּאמֶר לְאַבְרָם, יָדֹעַ

4 תֵּדַע, כִּי־גֵר יִהְיֶה זַרְעֲךָ, בְּאֶרֶץ לֹא לָהֶם, וַעֲבָדוּם וְעִנּוּ

5 אֹתָם. אַרְבַּע מֵאוֹת שָׁנָה: וְגַם אֶת־הַגּוֹי אֲשֶׁר יַעֲבֹדוּ, דָּן

6 אָנֹכִי. וְאַחֲרֵי־כֵן יֵצְאוּ, בִּרְכֻשׁ גָּדוֹל:

Covenant of Sacrifices In a vision Abraham heard the divine promise that he would become the father of a great nation. Abraham questioned God and said, "My wife Sarah is very old, and we have no children. I will die childless." And God replied, "Look at the heavens and count the stars; so numerous shall be your offspring and you shall also possess this land." Abraham continued to question, "How shall I know that I am to possess the land?" God answered, "Sacrifice several animals, and place them on the altar." Toward evening Abraham fell asleep and God once again spoke to him. "Your offspring will be strangers in a foreign land. They will be oppressed, and in the end they will go free." When the sun set and it was dark, there appeared a cloud of smoke, and a flaming torch passed between the pieces of the sacrifices. On that day Adonai made a *brit* (covenant) called the "Covenant of the Sacrifices," saying: "To your descendants I have given this land."

With great wealth. God impressed upon the Israelites that they need not be ashamed but should take the gold and silver of the Egyptians, since it was a justified payment for generations of slave labor. Germany, which imprisoned and murdered six million Jews in World War II, has also paid restitution for the slave labor of Jewish inmates in the Holocaust labor camps.

Blessed be the Eternal, who keeps the promise to Israel. Blessed is the Eternal. God foretold the end of slavery to Abraham at the <u>Covenant of Sacrifices.</u> The Eternal said to Abraham: "You and your children will be strangers in a land that is not their own. They will be enslaved there and will suffer for 400 years. The nation who will oppress them shall be punished. Afterward the Israelites will leave <u>with great wealth.</u>"

With great wealth. Some of the Egyptian people were friendly toward the Israelites and very much aware of the injustices against them. They were also fearful that some day the evil Pharaoh could just as well enslave them. As the Israelites left, the righteous Egyptians, as a sign of friendship, freely gave them gold and silver ornaments and clothing. These tokens of friendship and remorse were later used in building the sanctuary in the desert.

The reparations were freely given by repentant Egyptians, in contrast to the European reparations after World War II. It took threats and lawsuits for the Swiss, Germans, Italians, Poles, and French to return stolen Jewish property and bank deposits.

To its credit, the German government accepted responsibility for the Holocaust and has paid and is continuing to pay reparations to the government of Israel and to individual victims.

Cover the matzah, raise your wine cup, and say:

וְהִיא שֶׁעָמְדָה לַאֲבוֹתֵינוּ וְלֵנוּ. שֶׁלֹּא אֶחָד בִּלְבָד, עָמַד 1

עָלֵינוּ לְכַלּוֹתֵנוּ. אֶלָּא שֶׁבְּכָל דּוֹר וָדוֹר, עוֹמְדִים עָלֵינוּ 2

לְכַלּוֹתֵנוּ. וְהַקָּדוֹשׁ בָּרוּךְ הוּא מַצִּילֵנוּ מִיָּדָם: 3

Put down the wine cup, uncover the matzah, and continue:

צֵא וּלְמַד, מַה בִּקֵּשׁ לָבָן הָאֲרַמִּי לַעֲשׂוֹת לְיַעֲקֹב אָבִינוּ. 4

שֶׁפַּרְעֹה לֹא גָזַר אֶלָּא עַל־הַזְּכָרִים. וְלָבָן בִּקֵּשׁ לַעֲקֹר 5

אֶת־הַכֹּל. שֶׁנֶּאֱמַר: אֲרַמִּי אֹבֵד אָבִי, וַיֵּרֶד מִצְרַיְמָה. 6

וַיָּגָר שָׁם בִּמְתֵי מְעָט. וַיְהִי־שָׁם לְגוֹי גָּדוֹל, עָצוּם וָרָב: 7

An Aramean tried to destroy my father Laban the Aramean was the father of Jacob's two wives, Leah and Rachel. Laban took every opportunity to cheat his son-in-law Jacob. At the wedding ceremony Laban changed brides, so Jacob married Leah instead of Rachel. Jacob dearly loved Rachel, so he worked another seven years for Laban in order to be able to marry her.

The Torah tells us that Laban also cheated Jacob out of his rightful wages. At the end of 20 years, Jacob and his family, in the middle of the night, stole away to Canaan. Laban assembled a small army and chased after them. After seven days, he caught up with Jacob and angrily confronted him. That night God appeared to Laban and warned him not to interfere with Jacob and his family. So the next day Laban and Jacob negotiated a treaty of peace and friendship. If God had not frightened Laban, he would have kidnapped Jacob's children and stolen his property. Jacob's children would have been brought up as the children of Laban, the Aramean cheat. And then there would have been no Children of Israel. This means you.

Laban the Aramean The Haggadah points out that Laban's intentions against Israel were more sinister than those of Pharaoh. The Egyptian king used the Israelites as slaves to build the store cities of Pithom and Rameses, but "Laban sought to uproot everything." Laban tried to destroy the Jewish people by undermining Jacob's steadfast faith in God.

Cover the matzah, raise your wine cup, and say:
The promise made to our ancestors is also for us at this Seder.
Evil people more than once have tried to destroy the Jews.
In every generation there are those that seek to harm us. But
the Holy One saves us from their hands.

Put down the wine cup and continue:
I'll teach you what <u>Laban the Aramean</u> tried to do to our father
Jacob. While Pharaoh ordered death only against the male
children, Laban tried to destroy them all. The Torah says:
<u>An Aramean tried to destroy my father</u>: and he went down
to Egypt and lived there."
Raise the wine cup and say:
Few in number. There he became a great and mighty and
numerous nation.

Laban The story of Laban is a reminder to be on guard against "friends"
who appear to be trustworthy and sympathize with you. Behind your
back they may really be plotting and planning to harm you. Enemies in
disguise are very dangerous, for the victim is unaware of the coming
ambush. Laban masqueraded as Jacob's friend, but in actuality he was a
secret enemy. Cults and conversion societies use friendship tactics to
entice Jewish teens into their camp and brainwash them.

Aramean The land of Mesopotania is also known as Aram-Naharaim,
meaning the "land between two rivers": the Tigris and the Euphrates.
Starting in the time of the patriarch Abraham, the Arameans played a sig-
nificant role in the ancient history of the Jewish people. Aram was part of
the rich area now designated as the fertile crescent. The area today includes
Israel, Jordan, Lebanon, Syria, and Iraq. The Arameans came out of the
same Semitic people as the Hebrews, and were clearly related to them.

1 **וַיֵּרֶד מִצְרַיְמָה.** אָנוּס עַל פִּי הַדִּבּוּר. וַיָּגָר שָׁם. מְלַמֵּד שֶׁלֹּא

2 יָרַד יַעֲקֹב אָבִינוּ לְהִשְׁתַּקֵּעַ בְּמִצְרַיִם. אֶלָּא לָגוּר שָׁם.

3 שֶׁנֶּאֱמַר: וַיֹּאמְרוּ אֶל־פַּרְעֹה, לָגוּר בָּאָרֶץ בָּאנוּ, כִּי־אֵין

4 מִרְעֶה לַצֹּאן אֲשֶׁר לַעֲבָדֶיךָ, כִּי־כָבֵד הָרָעָב בְּאֶרֶץ כְּנָעַן.

5 וְעַתָּה, יֵשְׁבוּ־נָא עֲבָדֶיךָ בְּאֶרֶץ גֹּשֶׁן:

6 **בִּמְתֵי מְעָט.** כְּמָה שֶׁנֶּאֱמַר: בְּשִׁבְעִים נֶפֶשׁ, יָרְדוּ אֲבֹתֶיךָ

7 מִצְרָיְמָה. וְעַתָּה, שָׂמְךָ יְיָ אֱלֹהֶיךָ, כְּכוֹכְבֵי הַשָּׁמַיִם לָרֹב:

8 **וַיְהִי שָׁם לְגוֹי.** מְלַמֵּד שֶׁהָיוּ יִשְׂרָאֵל מְצֻיָּנִים שָׁם:

9 **גָּדוֹל עָצוּם.** כְּמָה שֶׁנֶּאֱמַר: וּבְנֵי יִשְׂרָאֵל, פָּרוּ וַיִּשְׁרְצוּ, וַיִּרְבּוּ

10 וַיַּעַצְמוּ, בִּמְאֹד מְאֹד. וַתִּמָּלֵא הָאָרֶץ אֹתָם:

Jacob did not go to Egypt to live there. Jacob (Israel) and his family were forced to go to Egypt because of the famine in Caanan. Jacob had every intention of returning to the Promised Land when the famine was over. Unfortunately, he died in Egypt, but on his deathbed he said to his children, "You must bury me with my family in the land of Canaan in the cave in the field of Machpelah." There he was buried with Abraham and Sarah, Isaac, Rebecca, and Leah. Israel also said to Joseph, "I am about to die, but God will be with you and bring you back to Canaan, the land of your ancestors." When Joseph died he made his brothers promise to return his body to Canaan.

Throughout the generations many Jews living in foreign countries have asked to be buried in Israel in the belief that the resurrection predicted by the prophet Ezekiel will take place there. In the words of Ezekiel, "I will open the graves of exile and cause you to rise again."

Famine It is hard for us to understand today how dreadful a famine can be, nor can we fully appreciate the constant concern of the ancients that they might soon have to face one. The people of ancient Egypt were dependent on the annual flooding of the Nile River to bring water for that year's crops. They had no way of knowing what the next year would bring, much less the next seven.

He went down to Egypt. Why did he go down to Egypt? Because he was driven by the Eternal's holy word.

He lived there. This teaches us that <u>Jacob, our father, did not go down to Egypt to live there</u> permanently, but only to stay for a short time. They said to Pharaoh, "We have come to live in Egypt only because there is no grass for the animals in the land of Canaan and there is a great <u>famine,</u> and now please allow your servants to live in the land of Goshen."

Few in number. The Torah says: "Your ancestors went down into Egypt <u>with seventy people.</u> Now the Eternal, your God, has made you as many as the stars in heaven."

<u>And there he became a nation.</u> This teaches us that Israel became a separate nation in Egypt.

Great and mighty. The Torah says: "And the Children of Israel were fruitful and increased and became very strong, so that the land was filled with them."

With seventy people Between the time of Joseph and the ascent of Rameses II to the Egyptian throne, nearly 400 years passed of which 210 years were spent in slavery. The Israelites had grown to a population of several hundred thousand. Rameses II was not only a new ruler, he was also the founder of a new dynasty. Joseph had served during the time of the Hyksos, or "Shepherd Kings." The Hyksos were friendly to the Hebrews and remembered Joseph and his deeds. Rameses II changed that policy and ignored Joseph's accomplishments for Egypt.

And there they became a nation. From this phrase we learn that during their sojourn in Egypt the Israelites retained their individuality and became a distinct nation. They did not adopt Egyptian names, they did not participate in Egyptian religious ceremonies, and they continued to speak Hebrew.

1 וָרֹב. כְּמָה שֶׁנֶּאֱמַר: רְבָבָה כְּצֶמַח הַשָּׂדֶה נְתַתִּיךְ, וַתִּרְבִּי,

2 וַתִּגְדְּלִי, וַתָּבֹאִי בַּעֲדִי עֲדָיִים. שָׁדַיִם נָכֹנוּ, וּשְׂעָרֵךְ צִמֵּחַ,

3 וְאַתְּ עֵרֹם וְעֶרְיָה:

4 **וַיָּרֵעוּ אֹתָנוּ הַמִּצְרִים** וַיְעַנּוּנוּ. וַיִּתְּנוּ עָלֵינוּ עֲבֹדָה קָשָׁה:

5 **וַיָּרֵעוּ אֹתָנוּ הַמִּצְרִים**, כְּמָה שֶׁנֶּאֱמַר: הָבָה נִתְחַכְּמָה לוֹ.

6 פֶּן־יִרְבֶּה וְהָיָה כִּי־תִקְרֶאנָה מִלְחָמָה, וְנוֹסַף גַּם־הוּא עַל־

7 שֹׂנְאֵינוּ, וְנִלְחַם־בָּנוּ וְעָלָה מִן־הָאָרֶץ:

8 **וַיְעַנּוּנוּ.** כְּמָה שֶׁנֶּאֱמַר: וַיָּשִׂימוּ עָלָיו שָׂרֵי מִסִּים לְמַעַן

9 עַנֹּתוֹ בְּסִבְלֹתָם: וַיִּבֶן עָרֵי מִסְכְּנוֹת לְפַרְעֹה, אֶת־פִּתֹם

10 וְאֶת־רַעַמְסֵס: וַיִּתְּנוּ עָלֵינוּ עֲבֹדָה קָשָׁה. כְּמָה שֶׁנֶּאֱמַר:

11 וַיַּעֲבִדוּ מִצְרַיִם אֶת־בְּנֵי יִשְׂרָאֵל בְּפָרֶךְ:

Yet you are naked and bare. After lots of hard work, the Jews in Spain, Russia, and Germany achieved success economically, socially, artistically, and politically. But history, especially Jewish history, teaches that success can sometimes be an illusion.

At first the Jewish newcomers were peddlers, small merchants, and craftsmen. After years of hard work many achieved success and climbed from rags to riches. After years of success the tide turned. Their wealth, and property were expropriated, and the riches turned to rags. They became "naked and bare."

The Egyptians were cruel to us. The Hebrew word *vayarehu* can also mean "they made us look evil." Joseph had a marvelous reputation and the Israelites were also good for the land of Egypt. Now, the new king, for some political reason, decided to strip the Jews of their reputation. Like other dictators, czars, and political despots, he began a propaganda campaign by circulating rumors that Jews were not trustworthy, killed children, spied for the enemy, poisoned wells, and were trying to take over the world.

And numerous. The Torah says: "I have increased you like the plants in the field and you have become numerous and flowered and become very beautiful. You are fully grown, yet <u>you are naked and bare.</u>"

<u>And the Egyptians were cruel to us</u> and they made us suffer. "They made us work hard."
And the Egyptians were cruel to us. The Torah says: "Come, let us deal cleverly with the Israelites or they will increase even more, and should a war start they will join our enemies and fight against us and leave Egypt."

<u>And they made us suffer.</u> The Torah says: "So the Egyptians placed taskmasters over them to crush them with cruelty; and they built the store cities of <u>Pithom and Rameses</u> for Pharaoh. "And they set upon us hard work." the Torah says, "And Egypt made the Children of Israel work very hard."

And they made us suffer. Throughout history the oppressed have identified their oppressor with Pharaoh and themselves with the Israelites. Such identification sustained the cause of the American Revolution against Britain. The festival of Passover activates the message of freedom not only for the Jewish people, but for all seekers of freedom.
The Liberty Bell in Philadelphia sounds and reverberates the biblical message, " Proclaim liberty throughout the land unto all the inhabitants thereof."

Pithom and Rameses Pharaoh decided to punish the Israelite slaves by forcing them to find their own straw for making bricks. He said, "You must produce the same quota of bricks with your own straw."
The foremen then complained to Moses, who complained to God and said, "Ever since I came to Pharaoh to speak in Your name, conditions for the Israelites have worsened." Then God said to Moses, "You shall see how I will punish Pharaoh. Say to the Children of Israel, I have heard their sufferings and I will free them from slavery in Egypt. I will deliver them from bondage, and I will redeem them with an outstretched hand and with miraculous signs."

1 **וַנִּצְעַק אֶל־יְיָ** אֱלֹהֵי אֲבֹתֵינוּ, וַיִּשְׁמַע יְיָ אֶת־קֹלֵנוּ, וַיַּרְא

2 אֶת־עָנְיֵנוּ, וְאֶת־עֲמָלֵנוּ, וְאֶת־לַחֲצֵנוּ:

3 **וַנִּצְעַק אֶל־יְיָ** אֱלֹהֵי אֲבוֹתֵינוּ. כְּמָה שֶׁנֶּאֱמַר: וַיְהִי בַיָּמִים

4 הָרַבִּים הָהֵם, וַיָּמָת מֶלֶךְ מִצְרַיִם, וַיֵּאָנְחוּ בְנֵי־יִשְׂרָאֵל מִן־

5 הָעֲבֹדָה וַיִּזְעָקוּ. וַתַּעַל שַׁוְעָתָם אֶל־הָאֱלֹהִים מִן־הָעֲבֹדָה:

6 וַיִּשְׁמַע יְיָ אֶת־קֹלֵנוּ. כְּמָה שֶׁנֶּאֱמַר: וַיִּשְׁמַע אֱלֹהִים אֶת־

7 נַאֲקָתָם. וַיִּזְכֹּר אֱלֹהִים אֶת־בְּרִיתוֹ, אֶת־אַבְרָהָם, אֶת־

8 יִצְחָק וְאֶת־יַעֲקֹב:

9 **וַיַּרְא אֶת־עָנְיֵנוּ.** זוֹ פְּרִישׁוּת דֶּרֶךְ אֶרֶץ. כְּמָה שֶׁנֶּאֱמַר: וַיַּרְא

10 אֱלֹהִים אֶת־בְּנֵי יִשְׂרָאֵל. וַיֵּדַע אֱלֹהִים:

And the Eternal heard our voice When God wanted to find a compassionate leader to lead the Israelites out of Egypt and save them from slavery, He decided to test Moses. Adonai watched Moses as he guarded his flock of sheep. A young lamb separated itself and ran away. Moses pursued the lamb, caught it, and gently lifted it into his arms and carried it all the way back to the flock. Seeing the kindness and concern that Moses had for the lamb, God knew that he would be a kind and compassionate leader for the Children of Israel.

Our misery Moses, the Egyptian prince, was raised by his real mother, Jochebed. She taught him all the laws and rules of Judaism. One day Moses left the palace to check on the conditions of his fellow Hebrews who were slaving at a construction site. From afar he spied a slavemaster beating an Israelite. Moses heard his cries of pain and intervened. But in the struggle Moses killed the Egyptian. The Hebrew escaped and excitedly told his people about being saved by Moses, the Egyptian prince. The next day someone informed the Pharaoh. The king could not allow the death to go unpunished, so he ordered the arrest of Moses. But someone warned Moses, and he escaped to Midian. Moses could have lived a life of luxury and power as a prince of Egypt. Yet when he saw the misery of his people, he did not stand by and do nothing. He acted courageously and defended his people.

So we cried to the Eternal, the God of our ancestors. And the Eternal heard our voice, and God saw our suffering in <u>our misery.</u>

So we cried to the Eternal, the God of our ancestors. The Torah says: "And it came to pass that the king of Egypt died, and the children of Israel groaned and cried out, and their tears came up to God."

<u>**And the Eternal heard our voice.**</u> The Torah says: "And God heard their groans and God remembered <u>His covenant with Abraham,</u> Isaac, and Jacob."

<u>**And the Eternal saw our suffering.**</u> This phrase refers to the separation of families. The Torah says: "And the Eternal saw the Children of Israel, and God understood their pain."

His covenant with Abraham The text repeats the phrase Abraham, Isaac and Jacob because these three personalities emphasize three important qualities upon which the world was founded. Abraham is symbolic of doing mitzvot of lovingkindness, Isaac represents the service of prayer, Jacob is a model for the study of the Torah.

And Eternal saw our suffering God looked down and saw the suffering of the Israelites. Our sages asked, "What else did the Holy One see? " And they answered, "God also saw Israelites helping and showing mercy to one another. When a strong Israelite completed his quota of bricks, he immediately turned and helped a weaker slave complete his quota. When God saw this, He said, 'These people are worthy to be shown mercy, for he who shows mercy must be shown mercy.' " As part of the 4,000-year-old tradition, Jews today continue to show mercy to those who for many reasons cannot complete their lives physically, mentally, and economically. Jews participate in and sponsor charitable institutions, hospitals, lending programs, homes for the aged, and schools to help those with special needs.

1 וְאֶת־עֲמָלֵנוּ. אֵלוּ הַבָּנִים. כְּמָה שֶׁנֶּאֱמַר: כָּל־הַבֵּן הַיִּלּוֹד

2 הַיְאֹרָה תַּשְׁלִיכֻהוּ, וְכָל־הַבַּת תְּחַיּוּן:

3 וְאֶת־לַחֲצֵנוּ. זוֹ הַדְּחַק. כְּמָה שֶׁנֶּאֱמַר: וְגַם־רָאִיתִי אֶת־

4 הַלַּחַץ, אֲשֶׁר מִצְרַיִם לֹחֲצִים אֹתָם:

5 **וַיּוֹצִאֵנוּ יְיָ מִמִּצְרַיִם**, בְּיָד חֲזָקָה, וּבִזְרֹעַ נְטוּיָה, וּבְמֹרָא גָּדֹל.

6 וּבְאֹתוֹת וּבְמֹפְתִים:

7 **וַיּוֹצִאֵנוּ יְיָ מִמִּצְרַיִם.** לֹא עַל־יְדֵי מַלְאָךְ. וְלֹא עַל־יְדֵי

8 שָׂרָף. וְלֹא עַל־יְדֵי שָׁלִיחַ. אֶלָּא הַקָּדוֹשׁ בָּרוּךְ הוּא

9 בִּכְבוֹדוֹ וּבְעַצְמוֹ. שֶׁנֶּאֱמַר: וְעָבַרְתִּי בְאֶרֶץ־מִצְרַיִם בַּלַּיְלָה

10 הַזֶּה. וְהִכֵּיתִי כָל־בְּכוֹר בְּאֶרֶץ מִצְרַיִם מֵאָדָם וְעַד־בְּהֵמָה.

11 וּבְכָל־אֱלֹהֵי מִצְרַיִם, אֶעֱשֶׂה שְׁפָטִים, אֲנִי יְיָ:

Every son that is born to you. The Egyptian princess found the child floating in a watertight basket. She knew that it was one of the Hebrew babies that her father, the Pharaoh, had condemned to be killed. The princess was also aware that anyone hiding a Hebrew baby would immediatly be put to death. Despite the danger, her feelings of love and respect for human life forced her to save the child. The princess acted out of the spirit of pity and righteousness.

During the Holocaust there were many Gentiles who risked their lives to save Jews from the Nazis. These non-Jews are called Righteous Gentiles. At the Yad Vashem memorial in Jerusalem, there is special section devoted to Righteous Gentiles who saved Jews despite the danger to themselves.

Every son that is born to you. The Hebrew midwives were instructed by the Egyptians to kill all newborn baby boys. The Talmud says that two of the midwives, Puah and Shifrah, risked their lives and hid the children from the Egyptians. As a reward for their heroism, the Eternal made them the founders of two great dynasties. Jochebed, the mother of Moses and Aaron, was Shifrah, and her descendants became the dynasty of the Kohanim (priests) and the Levites. Miriam, the sister of Moses and Aaron, was Puah, and she founded the dynasty of the House of David.

And our burden. This reminds us of the drowning of the sons.
As the Torah says: "Every son that is born to you
cast into the river, but you shall save every daughter."

And our oppression. This refers to the crushing of our lives, as
the Torah says: "And I have seen the cruelty with which
the Egyptians are crushing them."

And the Eternal brought us out of Egypt with a strong
hand and an outstretched arm and with great terror and
with miraculous signs and wonders.

And the Eternal brought us out of Egypt-not by a fiery
angel, and not by a messenger,but by Himself, in His glory, as
it is written:"I will pass through the land of Egypt on this
night, and I will attack all the firstborn in the land of Egypt
from man to beast, and I will execute judgment against all the
gods of Egypt. I am the Eternal."

And the Eternal brought us out of Egypt. Note that the Haggadah continually emphasizes God's role in freeing the Israelites from Egyptian slavery. Curiously, Moses the leader, the driving force of the Exodus, appears only once in the Haggadah. Why? The sages who composed the Haggadah wanted to make sure that succeeding generations seeking freedom would not wait for a leader comparable to Moses. Each generation, in each period, has the ability to generate its own political and religious freedom fighters. In our generation, leaders such as David ben-Gurion and Golda Meier helped establish the State of Israel. Natan Sharansky and Alexander Lerner fought and suffered to free the Jews of Russia. Hannah Senesch and Rabbi Leo Baeck were instrumental in the fight against Nazi Germany during the Holocaust. God alone was the hero of the Exodus. It was God alone who sent Moses and performed the miracles and set the stage for the Exodus.

Every son that is born to you. With tears running down her cheeks, Jochebed placed her tiny son in a basket and floated him down the river Nile. Miriam, his sister, watched from the reeds as the Egyptian princess found the baby. Miriam bravely dared to speak to the Egyptian princess and arranged for Jochebed to bring up the baby, her own son. Hebrew midwives similarly risked their lives by not drowning the Israelite children as Pharaoh decreed. The rabbis say that because of the bravery of all these brave women, Israel was freed from slavery.

1 וְעָבַרְתִּי בְאֶרֶץ־מִצְרַיִם בַּלַּיְלָה הַזֶּה, אֲנִי וְלֹא מַלְאָךְ.

2 וְהִכֵּיתִי כָל־בְּכוֹר בְּאֶרֶץ מִצְרַיִם, אֲנִי וְלֹא שָׂרָף. וּבְכָל־

3 אֱלֹהֵי מִצְרַיִם אֶעֱשֶׂה שְׁפָטִים, אֲנִי וְלֹא הַשָּׁלִיחַ. אֲנִי יְיָ,

4 אֲנִי הוּא וְלֹא אַחֵר:

5 בְּיָד חֲזָקָה. זוֹ הַדֶּבֶר. כְּמָה שֶׁנֶּאֱמַר: הִנֵּה יַד־יְיָ הוֹיָה,

6 בְּמִקְנְךָ אֲשֶׁר בַּשָּׂדֶה, בַּסּוּסִים בַּחֲמֹרִים בַּגְּמַלִּים, בַּבָּקָר

7 וּבַצֹּאן. דֶּבֶר כָּבֵד מְאֹד:

And I will pass through the land of Egypt this night. I and not an angel. And I will punish the firstborn in the land of Egypt. I and not a fiery angel. And I will execute judgment against all the gods of Egypt. I and not a messenger. I am the Eternal."

With a strong hand. This refers to the cattle disease, as the Torah says: "The hand of the Eternal will smite the cattle in the field, the horses, the donkeys, the camels, the oxen and the sheep with a great plague."

1 **וּבִזְרֹעַ נְטוּיָה** זוֹ הַחֶרֶב. כְּמָה שֶׁנֶּאֱמַר. וְחַרְבּוֹ שְׁלוּפָה בְּיָדוֹ,

2 נְטוּיָה עַל־יְרוּשָׁלָ͏ִם:

3 **וּבְמֹרָא גָּדוֹל.** זוֹ גִּלוּי שְׁכִינָה. כְּמָה שֶׁנֶּאֱמַר: אוֹ הֲנִסָּה

4 אֱלֹהִים, לָבוֹא לָקַחַת לוֹ גוֹי מִקֶּרֶב גּוֹי, בְּמַסֹּת

5 בְּאֹתֹת וּבְמוֹפְתִים וּבְמִלְחָמָה, וּבְיָד חֲזָקָה וּבִזְרוֹעַ נְטוּיָה,

6 וּבְמוֹרָאִים גְּדֹלִים. כְּכֹל אֲשֶׁר־עָשָׂה לָכֶם, יְיָ אֱלֹהֵיכֶם,

7 בְּמִצְרַיִם לְעֵינֶיךָ:

8 **וּבְאֹתוֹת.** זֶה הַמַּטֶּה. כְּמָה שֶׁנֶּאֱמַר: וְאֶת־הַמַּטֶּה הַזֶּה, תִּקַּח

9 בְּיָדֶךָ. אֲשֶׁר תַּעֲשֶׂה־בּוֹ אֶת־הָאֹתֹת:

10 **וּבְמוֹפְתִים.** זֶה הַדָּם. כְּמָה שֶׁנֶּאֱמַר: וְנָתַתִּי מוֹפְתִים, בַּשָּׁמַיִם

וּבָאָרֶץ.

And with signs Moses killed an Egyptian taskmaster and fled to the land of Midian. There he became a shepherd and married Zipporah, the daughter of Jethro. One day, as Moses was tending his sheep, he noticed a burning bush. The red flames crackled and leaped high into the air. Moses was transfixed, and he heard a voice from the midst of the burning bush: "Moses, Moses!" He listened and said, "Here I am." The mysterious voice said, "Moses, do not come closer; remove your shoes from your feet, for you are now standing on holy ground." And the voice from the bush continued: "I am the God of your father, the God of Abraham, of Isaac, and of Jacob. I have seen the wrongs and the cruelty that My people are suffering in Egypt. I am coming to set them free. I will send you to Pharaoh, and you shall lead My people out of Egypt." Moses hid his face and said in fear; "Who am I that I should go to Pharaoh? What shall I say to him?" And God said, "I will be with you. I will tell you what to say."

And with an outstretched arm. This refers to the sword, as the Torah says: "God's drawn sword stretched over Jerusalem."

And with great terror. This refers to the Revelation of the Eternal to Israel, as the Torah says: "Has any god ever succeeded to remove one nation from the midst of another nation, and with trials <u>and signs, and wonders,</u> and battle, and by a strong hand and an outstretched arm, and by deeds of terror?"

<u>**And with signs.**</u> This refers to the rod, as it is written: "Take this rod in your hand, and with it perform the signs."

And wonders. This refers to the plague of blood, as it is written: "And I will show wonders in the heavens and on earth."

And signs, and wonders. At the burning bush, Moses's rod turned into a snake. And then back again into a rod. His hand turned leprous and then instantly cured itself. And God said, "Use your rod and do the signs when you reach Egypt." God sent Moses to free the Israelites from Egypt. Moses said to God, "But the Hebrews will not listen to me. That miraculous rod was used to perform miracles in the palace of the Pharaoh. Moses stretched his rod over the Red Sea, and it created a path to the other side. Later the rod was used by Moses to strike a rock and get water for the thirsty Israelites. Moses also used the rod to win a great victory over the Amalekites. Before Moses died he handed the rod over to Joshua. The Midrash says that the rod was a limb from the Tree of Knowledge in the Garden of Eden. God's special holy name was engraved on the rod.

Spill three drops of wine, one for each of the disasters.

1. <u>BLOOD</u> *Dam* **דָּם**

2. FIRE *Va-Esh* **וָאֵשׁ.**

3. PILLARS OF SMOKE *Ve-Timrot Ashen* **וְתִימְרוֹת עָשָׁן**

1 דָּבָר אַחֵר. בְּיָד חֲזָקָה שְׁתַּיִם. וּבִזְרֹעַ נְטוּיָה שְׁתַּיִם. וּבְמֹרָא
2 גָּדֹל שְׁתַּיִם. וּבְאֹתוֹת שְׁתַּיִם. וּבְמֹפְתִים שְׁתַּיִם: אֵלוּ עֶשֶׂר
3 מַכּוֹת שֶׁהֵבִיא הַקָּדוֹשׁ בָּרוּךְ הוּא עַל־הַמִּצְרִים בְּמִצְרָיִם.
4 וְאֵלּוּ הֵן:

Blood The Nile is the world's longest river. It starts deep in the heart of Africa and flows northward for 4,180 miles to the Mediterranean Sea. It is the lifeline of Egypt. The lifegiving waters of the Nile have created a farming area about 15 miles wide where plants and people thrive. Egypt is completely surrounded by deserts, except for this fertile strip of land. In Egypt, the Nile rises each year and waters the land. This is what made Egypt a prosperous country, although little rain fell. Therefore, the Egyptians worshipped the river. This explains why God deliberately chose the Nile as His first target. What happened to the waters of the Nile during the plagues? Perhaps some poisonous organism affected the water and caused the catastrophe. Was it a miracle? Very definitely! The waters were poisoned and the plague occurred at the exact time that Moses predicted.

Spill three drops of wine, one for each of the disasters.

1. **BLOOD** *Dam*

2. FIRE *Va-Esh*

3. PILLARS OF SMOKE
Ve-Timrot Ashen

Another interpretation is as follows: "With a strong hand" refers to two plagues; "with an outstretched arm," two plagues; "with great terror," two plagues; "with signs," two plagues; and "with wonders" refers to two plagues. All together we have <u>ten plagues</u> with which the Holy One punished the Egyptians in Egypt, and they are as follows:

Ten plagues The ten plagues that afflicted Egypt can be divided into three groups: earthy, atmospheric, and godly. The first six plagues happened on the earth: bloody water, frogs, lice, beasts, cattle disease, and boils. The next three plagues were atmospheric: hail, locusts brought by the winds, and darkness. God wanted Pharaoh to see the error of his ways and let the Hebrews go peacefully. So God sent the first nine plagues as a warning. God was merciful and did not wish to send destruction upon the innocent people of Egypt. But, after the ninth plague, God's patience was exhausted, so He sent the tenth and worst plague, the death of the firstborn.

Makot: plagues The plagues sent by God to punish the Egyptians correspond to their cruel actions against the Israelites. Because the Israelites were forced to draw water for the Egyptians, the water was changed to blood. Because the Egyptians forced the Israelites to catch fish for them, the rivers were filled with frogs. Because the Egyptians forced the Israelites to care for their flocks, the animals were struck down by disease. The tenth plague, the killing of the firstborn, was a punishment for Pharaoh's order to murder the boy children of the Israelites.

Spill a drop of wine for each of the ten plagues:

1. דָּם *Dam*

2. צְפַרְדֵּעַ *Tzfarde'ah*

3. כִּנִּים *Kinim*

4. עָרוֹב *Arov*

5. דֶּבֶר *Dever*

6. שְׁחִין *Shchin*

7. בָּרָד *Barad*

8. אַרְבֶּה *Arbeh*

9. חֹשֶׁךְ *Choshech*

10. מַכַּת בְּכוֹרוֹת *Makat b'chorot*

Rabbi Judah would refer to the ten plagues by their Hebrew initials:
Spill three drops of wine:

דְּצַ"ךְ עֲדַ"שׁ בְּאַחַ"ב

Drops of wine At the Passover Seder we celebrate the freedom of our ancestors from Egyptian slavery. Each person at the Seder spills out a drop of wine from their wine cup at the mention of each of the plagues. Some say that the drops of wine are tears of regret that freedom had to be purchased through the death of Egyptians.

Barad: hail The fact that hail did not rain down upon Goshen was a great miracle. Since the hail came down from the atmosphere, it was truly a miraculous act to isolate an area and free it from damage.

Chosech: darkness The darkness was so thick that it actually could be felt. According to some of the commentators, the blackout was so great that even of lighting could not penetrate the darkness.
Despite the fact that the Israelites lived near the Egyptians, they were not affected by the plague of darkness.

Spill a <u>drop of wine</u> for each of the ten plagues:

1. BLOOD *Dam*

2. FROGS *Tzfarde'ah*

3. VERMIN *Kinim*

4. WILD BEASTS *Arov*

5. PESTILENCE *Dever*

6. BOILS *Shchin*

7. <u>HAIL *Barad*</u>

8. LOCUSTS *Arbeh*

9. <u>DARKNESS *Choshech*</u>

10. SLAYING OF THE
FIRST BORN
Makat b'chorot

<u>Rabbi Judah</u> would refer to the ten plagues by their Hebrew initials:
Spill three drops of wine:

D'TZACH ADASH B'ACHAV

Rabbi Judah Rabbi Judah, a wise and gentle man, could not bring himself to recite the plagues. Even though the Egyptians were enemies, he felt that they were still God's creations. Since it pained him to recite the plagues, he formed the first letters of each plague into the three-word combination: D'TZACH, ADASH, B'ACHAV.

1 **רַבִּי יוֹסֵי הַגְּלִילִי אוֹמֵר:** מִנַּֽיִן אַתָּה אוֹמֵר, שֶׁלָּקוּ הַמִּצְרִים

2 בְּמִצְרַֽיִם עֶֽשֶׂר מַכּוֹת, וְעַל־הַיָּם, לָקוּ חֲמִשִּׁים מַכּוֹת

3 בְּמִצְרַֽיִם מָה הוּא אוֹמֵר: וַיֹּאמְרוּ הַחַרְטֻמִּם אֶל־פַּרְעֹה,

4 אֶצְבַּע אֱלֹהִים הוּא. וְעַל־הַיָּם מָה הוּא אוֹמֵר: וַיַּרְא

5 יִשְׂרָאֵל אֶת־הַיָּד הַגְּדֹלָה, אֲשֶׁר עָשָׂה יְיָ בְּמִצְרַֽיִם, וַיִּֽירְאוּ

6 הָעָם אֶת־יְיָ. וַיַּאֲמִֽינוּ בַּיָי, וּבְמֹשֶׁה עַבְדּוֹ: כַּמָּה לָקוּ

7 בָאֶצְבַּע, עֶֽשֶׂר מַכּוֹת. אֱמוֹר מֵעַתָּה: בְּמִצְרַֽיִם, לָקוּ עֶֽשֶׂר

8 מַכּוֹת, וְעַל־הַיָּם, לָקוּ חֲמִשִּׁים מַכּוֹת:

9 **רַבִּי אֱלִיעֶֽזֶר אוֹמֵר:** מִנַּֽיִן שֶׁכָּל־מַכָּה וּמַכָּה, שֶׁהֵבִיא הַקָּדוֹשׁ

10 בָּרוּךְ הוּא עַל־הַמִּצְרִים בְּמִצְרַֽיִם, הָיְתָה שֶׁל אַרְבַּע מַכּוֹת

11 שֶׁנֶּאֱמַר: יְשַׁלַּח־בָּם חֲרוֹן אַפּוֹ, עֶבְרָה וָזַֽעַם וְצָרָה. מִשְׁלַֽחַת

12 מַלְאֲכֵי רָעִים. עֶבְרָה אַחַת. וָזַֽעַם שְׁתַּֽיִם. וְצָרָה שָׁלֹשׁ.

13 מִשְׁלַֽחַת מַלְאֲכֵי רָעִים אַרְבַּע. אֱמוֹר מֵעַתָּה: בְּמִצְרַֽיִם,

14 לָקוּ אַרְבָּעִים מַכּוֹת, וְעַל־הַיָּם, לָקוּ מָאתַֽיִם מַכּוֹת:

Rabbi Jose the Galilean was a talmudic scholar (2nd century C.E.) and a pupil of Rabbis Tarfon and Akiva. Jose was regarded as a wonder worker whose prayers for rain were effective. His decisions on Jewish legal issues are scattered throughout the Talmud. Jose's tomb is located near Sefad in the Galilee.

This is the finger of God Once again, Moses and Aaron went to Pharaoh and told him God had said that he must let the Children of Israel go out of Egypt. The cruel king laughed at them and replied, "I know nothing of this God of yours. Who is he to tell the mighty Pharaoh of all Egypt what to do? I shall not let the Israelite slaves go free." "Watch and you will see how mighty is our God," said Moses. Then he turned to Aaron and said, "Cast the rod on the ground." Pharaoh drew back in amazement, for the rod had turned into a snake. The angry king called his magicians and wise men and ordered them to cast their rods on the ground. Their rods also turned into snakes. But the rod of Moses ate up all the others, and then became a rod again.

Rabbi Jose the Galilean said: "How can you prove that after the ten plagues in Egypt the Egyptians were smitten with fifty plagues at the Red Sea? Of one of the plagues in Egypt it is written, 'The magicians said to Pharaoh, "This is the finger of God," while at the Red Sea it is written, 'And Israel saw the great hand which the Lord had shown against Egypt, and the people feared the Eternal and believed in the Eternal and in His servant Moses.' If one finger of God in Egypt caused ten plagues, we may thus logically calculate that the whole hand of the Eternal at the Red Sea caused fifty plagues."

Rabbi Eliezer said: "How can you prove that every plague which the Holy One brought upon the Egyptians in Egypt was fourfold in character? It is written: 'He sent against the Egyptians in his burning anger, wrath, indignation, trouble, and the Messengers of Evil.' 'Wrath' is one, 'indignation' two; 'trouble' three; 'the Messengers of Evil' four. If, then, in Egypt they were smitten with ten fourfold plagues, making forty, then following the earlier interpretation, at the Red Sea they suffered two hundred plagues."

His servant Moses The Torah tells us that Moses had a speech defect, yet God chose him to be the leader of Israel. Why? God's choice teaches us that a true leader does not have to be a polished orator or a demagogue who can arouse anger. A true leader is a charismatic personality who can inspire people to the state of "we will obey and we will hear," the words of the Israelites when they were given the Torah at Sinai. This is the only place in the Haggadah where the name of Moses is mentioned.

1 **רַבִּי עֲקִיבָא אוֹמֵר:** מִנַּיִן שֶׁכָּל־מַכָּה וּמַכָּה שֶׁהֵבִיא הַקָּדוֹשׁ

2 בָּרוּךְ הוּא עַל־הַמִּצְרִים בְּמִצְרַיִם, הָיְתָה שֶׁל חָמֵשׁ מַכּוֹת?

3 שֶׁנֶּאֱמַר: וְיְשַׁלַּח־בָּם חֲרוֹן אַפּוֹ עֶבְרָה וָזַעַם וְצָרָה. מִשְׁלַחַת

4 מַלְאֲכֵי רָעִים. חֲרוֹן אַפּוֹ אַחַת. עֶבְרָה שְׁתַּיִם. וָזַעַם שָׁלֹשׁ.

5 וְצָרָה אַרְבַּע. מִשְׁלַחַת מַלְאֲכֵי רָעִים חָמֵשׁ. אֱמוֹר מֵעַתָּה:

6 בְּמִצְרַיִם, לָקוּ חֲמִשִּׁים מַכּוֹת, וְעַל הַיָּם, לָקוּ חֲמִשִּׁים

7 וּמָאתַיִם מַכּוֹת:

Rabbi Akiva Rabbi Akiva was one of the leaders who urged the revolt
against Rome. As its commander he chose Simon bar Kozeba, who had
organized a guerrilla force to fight against the Romans.
The rabbis supported Bar Kozeba and renamed him Shimon Bar Kochba
("Son of a Star.") Akiva came to believe that Bar Kochba might be the
Messiah sent by God to restore the independence of the Jewish people. At
first Bar Kochba was victorious and managed to recapture Jerusalem.
Sadly, Judea had only two short years of independence. In 135 C.E. Bar
Kochba and his brave warriors made a final stand at Betar, and in the end
the fortress and all the soldiers were killed. Rabbi Akiva was condemned to
be skinned alive. With his dying breath he proclaimed "Shema Yisrael,
Hear O Israel, Adonai is our God, Adonai is One."

<u>Rabbi Akiva said:</u> "How can you show that every plague which the Holy One, blessed be He, brought upon the Egyptians in Egypt was fivefold in character? It is written: 'He sent against the Egyptians in His burning anger, wrath, indignation, trouble, and the Messengers of Evil.' 'His burning anger' is one; 'wrath' is two, 'indignation' three; 'trouble' four; 'the Messengers of Evil' five. Thus, if in Egypt the Egyptians were smitten with five tenfold plagues, making fifty, then at the Red Sea they suffered two hundred and fifty plagues."

DAYENU

|---|---|
1	כַּמָּה מַעֲלוֹת טוֹבוֹת לַמָּקוֹם עָלֵינוּ:
2	אִלּוּ הוֹצִיאָנוּ מִמִּצְרַיִם,
3	וְלֹא־עָשָׂה בָהֶם שְׁפָטִים,	דַּיֵּנוּ:
4	אִלּוּ עָשָׂה בָהֶם שְׁפָטִים,
5	וְלֹא־עָשָׂה בֵאלֹהֵיהֶם,	דַּיֵּנוּ:
6	אִלּוּ עָשָׂה בֵאלֹהֵיהֶם,
7	וְלֹא־הָרַג אֶת־בְּכוֹרֵיהֶם,	דַּיֵּנוּ:
8	אִלּוּ הָרַג אֶת־בְּכוֹרֵיהֶם,
9	וְלֹא־נָתַן לָנוּ אֶת־מָמוֹנָם,	דַּיֵּנוּ:
10	אִלּוּ נָתַן לָנוּ אֶת־מָמוֹנָם,
11	וְלֹא־קָרַע לָנוּ אֶת־הַיָּם,	דַּיֵּנוּ:
12	אִלּוּ קָרַע לָנוּ אֶת־הַיָּם,
13	וְלֹא־הֶעֱבִירָנוּ בְתוֹכוֹ בֶּחָרָבָה,	דַּיֵּנוּ:

Dayenu The Dayenu poem has 15 sections. The number 15 is often found in Jewish prayer.
1. Passover starts on the 15th day of the month of Nisan.
2. The priestly benediction consists of 15 words.

DAYENU

We must be thankful to God for all the wonderful and miraculous things done for us.

Had the Eternal brought us out from Egypt,
And not punished the Egyptians,
For us it was miraculous

Dayenu

Had the Eternal punished the Egyptians,
And not destroyed their idols,
For us it was miraculous

Dayenu

Had the Eternal killed their firstborn,
And not given us their wealth,
For us it was miraculous

Dayenu

Had the Eternal given us their wealth,
And not split *the Red Sea* for us,
For us it was miraculous   *Dayenu*

Had the Eternal split the sea for us,
And not brought us to safety,
For us it was miraculous

Dayenu

Had the Eternal brought us to safety,
And not drowned our enemies,
For us it was miraculous   *Dayenu*

The Red Sea It is not certain where the Israelites crossed into the wilderness of Sinai. Biblical scholars suggest three possible routes. The sea mentioned in the biblical account, the Yam Suf or Reed Sea, may have been an extensive bay of either the Mediterranean or the Red Sea, or more likely, the Bitter Lakes in the center of the lowlands now occupied by the Suez Canal. The Bitter Lakes, so called because of the high percentage of alkali salts in their water, were then, as they are today, very shallow in certain parts. It is entirely possible, as the Bible tells us, that a strong wind pushed the waters toward one end of the lake, thus lowering the sea level slightly at the other end. Where the lake bottom is exposed to the hot desert air, it becomes a surface of dried and cracked mud, topped by a layer of glistening salt.

1 אִלּוּ הֶעֱבִירָנוּ בְּתוֹכוֹ בֶּחָרָבָה,

2 וְלֹא־שִׁקַּע צָרֵינוּ בְּתוֹכוֹ, דַּיֵּנוּ:

3 אִלּוּ שִׁקַּע צָרֵינוּ בְּתוֹכוֹ,

4 וְלֹא־סִפֵּק צָרְכֵּנוּ בַּמִּדְבָּר אַרְבָּעִים שָׁנָה, דַּיֵּנוּ:

5 אִלּוּ סִפֵּק צָרְכֵּנוּ בַּמִּדְבָּר אַרְבָּעִים שָׁנָה,

6 וְלֹא־הֶאֱכִילָנוּ אֶת־הַמָּן, דַּיֵּנוּ:

7 אִלּוּ הֶאֱכִילָנוּ אֶת־הַמָּן,

8 וְלֹא־נָתַן לָנוּ אֶת־הַשַּׁבָּת, דַּיֵּנוּ:

9 אִלּוּ נָתַן לָנוּ אֶת הַשַּׁבָּת,

10 וְלֹא קֵרְבָנוּ לִפְנֵי הַר־סִינַי, דַּיֵּנוּ:

11 אִלּוּ קֵרְבָנוּ לִפְנֵי הַר־סִינַי,

12 וְלֹא־נָתַן לָנוּ אֶת־הַתּוֹרָה, דַּיֵּנוּ:

13 אִלּוּ נָתַן לָנוּ אֶת־הַתּוֹרָה,

14 וְלֹא־הִכְנִיסָנוּ לְאֶרֶץ יִשְׂרָאֵל, דַּיֵּנוּ:

15 אִלּוּ הִכְנִיסָנוּ לְאֶרֶץ יִשְׂרָאֵל,

16 וְלֹא־בָנָה לָנוּ אֶת־בֵּית הַבְּחִירָה, דַּיֵּנוּ:

And not drowned our enemies. Pharaoh regretted his decision to allow the Hebrew slaves to leave. So he mobilized 600 war chariots and thousands of foot soldiers and chased after them. When the Israelites saw the approaching army, they cried, "Moses, did you bring us out of Egypt to die in the desert?" Then Moses stretched his rod over the sea and a dry path opened. Without hesitation the Israelites quickly marched on the dry land to the other side of the Red Sea. Pharaoh's chariots galloped right into the sea after them. Then God said to Moses, "Stretch your rod once more over the sea so that the waters will return to their proper place." With a mighty roar the walls of water came tumbling down and all the Egyptians were drowned. At last, after 210 years of slavery, the Israelites were free.

Had the Eternal drowned our enemies,
  And not cared for us in the desert for 40 years,
    For us it was miraculous   *Dayenu*

Had the Eternal cared for us in the desert for 40 years,
  And not fed us manna,
    For us it was miraculous   *Dayenu*

Had the Eternal fed us <u>manna:</u>
  And not given us the Sabbath,
    For us it was miraculous   *Dayenu*

Had the Eternal given us the Sabbath,
  And not brought us to Mount Sinai
    For us it was miraculous   *Dayenu*

Had the Eternal brought us to Mount Sinai,
  And not given us the Torah
    For us it was miraculous   *Dayenu*

Had the Eternal given us the Torah,
  And not brought us into the land of Israel,
    For us it was miraculous   *Dayenu*

Had the Eternal brought us to the land of Israel,
  And not built for us the Holy Temple,
    For us it was miraculous   *Dayenu*

Had the Eternal drowned our enemies When the angels witnessed the miracle of the parting of the waters of the Sea of Reeds, so that the Israelites could cross on dry land, they began to sing happy songs of praise to God. But God did not allow them to rejoice. "The Egyptians are also My creations," He said. "Do not sing while My creatures are dying."

Manna To this day, when someone talks about something good coming in abundance and completely unexpected, they say, "It was like manna from heaven." The Torah says that when the Israelites awoke, the ground was covered with manna. Where did it come from? Some speculate that a certain insect that lives on trees gives off a large drop of liquid from its egg sac. When it comes out it is very white. The taste of these grains is very sweet and closely fits the description of the manna given in the Torah. It was like coriander seed, white, and was sweet tasting. The Arabs who live in the desert called this substance *man min sama.*
  In Hebrew that would be *man min shamayim,* or "manna from heaven."

1 **עַל אַחַת** כַּמָּה וְכַמָּה, טוֹבָה כְפוּלָה וּמְכֻפֶּלֶת, לַמָּקוֹם עָלֵינוּ.

2 שֶׁהוֹצִיאָנוּ מִמִּצְרַיִם, וְעָשָׂה בָהֶם שְׁפָטִים,

3 וְעָשָׂה בֵאלֹהֵיהֶם, וְהָרַג אֶת־בְּכוֹרֵיהֶם,

4 וְנָתַן לָנוּ אֶת־מָמוֹנָם, וְקָרַע לָנוּ אֶת־הַיָּם,

5 וְהֶעֱבִירָנוּ בְתוֹכוֹ בֶּחָרָבָה, וְשִׁקַּע צָרֵינוּ בְּתוֹכוֹ,

6 וְסִפֵּק צָרְכֵּנוּ בַּמִּדְבָּר אַרְבָּעִים שָׁנָה, וְהֶאֱכִילָנוּ אֶת־הַמָּן,

7 וְנָתַן לָנוּ אֶת־הַשַּׁבָּת, וְקֵרְבָנוּ לִפְנֵי הַר־סִינַי,

8 וְנָתַן לָנוּ אֶת־הַתּוֹרָה, וְהִכְנִיסָנוּ לְאֶרֶץ יִשְׂרָאֵל,

9 וּבָנָה לָנוּ אֶת־בֵּית הַבְּחִירָה לְכַפֵּר עַל־כָּל־עֲוֹנוֹתֵינוּ.

Manna When God gave the Israelites twice as much manna on the sixth day and it did not spoil the next morning, they understood the meaning of the Sabbath even better. In doing so, God said to them, "I want you to rest and make this day holy to Me, and I in turn will provide for you on the seventh day without any effort on your part."

In the years that followed, Israel realized that it was always possible to have a surplus for the Sabbath, and that if they obeyed God's command, God would provide them with a surplus that would permit them to rest and make the day holy. This went on for forty years. Until Israel had learned fully this lesson.

It is one that we can learn today, for if humans are replenished physically and spiritually on the Sabbath, they will be able to produce more during the week and will not have to work on the holy day of Shabbat.

The Land of Israel A clay tablet written in Babylonian cuneiform by a terrified Egyptian governor in Canaan begs the Pharaoh for help, saying: "The Khabiru [Hebrews] are taking the cities of the king. No ruler remains to the king, my lord; all is lost." The king of Egypt to whom he wrote this letter was Ikhnaton, at a time when the Egyptian empire in Asia was falling to pieces. This letter is one of a group of 300 cuneiform letters found in one of the rooms of Iknaton's palace at Tel-el Amarna, one of the oldest bodies of correspondence in the world. Some scholars are of the opinion that the Khabiru were the Hebrews. The tablets of Tel Amarna, dating from 1415 B.C.E., refer to one of the stages of the Israelite conquest of Canaan.

The Eternal has done all these wonderful things for us.

The Eternal took us out of Egypt,
and punished the Egyptians.
The Eternal destroyed their idols,
and killed their firstborn.
The Eternal gave us their treasures,
and divided the sea.
The Eternal led us across on dry land,
and drowned the Egyptians.
The Eternal took care of us in the desert for 40
years and fed us the <u>manna</u>.
The Eternal gave us the Sabbath,
and brought us to Mount Sinai.
The Eternal gave us <u>the Torah</u>,
and brought us to <u>the land of Israel</u>.
The Eternal built the Holy Temple,
where we could atone for our sins.

Manna How did the manna test the faith of the Israelites? The Torah tells us that the manna could not be stored, for it would spoil overnight. The Israelites had no method of storing food for a day if for some reason the manna from heaven did not appear. Only true faith allowed them to have any peace of mind for the next day's meal.

The Torah When God gave the Torah, no bird sang, no fowl flew, the sea did not roar, and no creature spoke. Even the angels stopped singing their praises of God. The entire world was silent. Only the voice of God could be heard, saying, "I am the Lord your God." The Torah is the most important Jewish religious book. It contains the basic information about the holiday of Passover. Second only to the Torah, in Judaism's rich library of literature, is the Talmud. The most important source for the laws of Passover is found in the Talmud in Tractate Pesachim. One of the most authoritative texts which contains the laws of Passover, is the *Shulchan Aruch* of Joseph Karo, was compiled in the 16th century.

1 רַבָּן גַּמְלִיאֵל הָיָה אוֹמֵר: כָּל־שֶׁלֹּא־אָמַר שְׁלֹשָׁה דְבָרִים

2 אֵלּוּ בַּפֶּסַח, לֹא־יָצָא יְדֵי חוֹבָתוֹ. וְאֵלּוּ הֵן:

1. פֶּסַח *The Passover Offering* (Pesach)

2. מַצָּה *The Matzah*

3. וּמָרוֹר *The Bitter Herbs* (Maror)

Point to the shankbone and say:

3 פֶּסַח שֶׁהָיוּ אֲבוֹתֵינוּ אוֹכְלִים, בִּזְמַן שֶׁבֵּית־הַמִּקְדָּשׁ קַיָּם,

4 עַל־שׁוּם מָה? עַל־שׁוּם, שֶׁפָּסַח הַקָּדוֹשׁ בָּרוּךְ הוּא, עַל־

5 בָּתֵּי אֲבוֹתֵינוּ בְּמִצְרָיִם. שֶׁנֶּאֱמַר: וַאֲמַרְתֶּם זֶבַח־פֶּסַח הוּא

6 לַייָ, אֲשֶׁר פָּסַח עַל־בָּתֵּי בְנֵי־יִשְׂרָאֵל בְּמִצְרַיִם, בְּנָגְפּוֹ

7 אֶת־מִצְרַיִם, וְאֶת־בָּתֵּינוּ הִצִּיל. וַיִּקֹּד הָעָם וַיִּשְׁתַּחֲווּ:

The Passover offering The Israelite families who sprinkled the blood of the lamb on their doorposts put their lives in danger. The lamb was one of the sacred gods of Egypt. Any Israelite caught sacrificing a lamb would most certainly be killed. The Israelites, who believed in God, performed the sacrifice, and God saved them from the Egyptians.

Why do we eat bitter herbs? Why do we recite the matzah section, which is a reminder of freedom, before the bitter herbs, which are a reminder of slavery? The sequence should be reversed, since bondage came before redemption. The order teaches us that only after the Israelites tasted freedom did they begin to understand the degradation of slavery. A slave becomes accustomed to misery and is not aware of his degradation. Only when people become free do they understand the value of freedom. In our time we have seen the demise of communism and the death of numerous dictatorships and the growth of democracy and freedom all over the world.

Rabbi Gamliel used to say: To fulfill your duty on Passover you must explain the following three symbols:

1. *The Passover Offering* (*Pesach*)

2. *The Matzah*

3. *The Bitter Herbs* (*Maror*)

Point to the shankbone and say:
Pesach Why did our ancestors eat the Passover sacrifice in Temple days? Because the Eternal "passed over" (*pasach*) the homes of our ancestors in Egypt. The Torah says, "It is a Passover offering because the Eternal 'passed over' the homes of the Children of Israel in Egypt."

Matzah This is unleavened bread prepared from flour made from grain that was not washed and was milled under supervision, completely protected from contact with water. Matzah must be prepared only with water that has been stored overnight. Stored water slows the process of leavening. The matzah dough is kneaded either by hand or by machine, in a cool room, since heat may cause leavening. The dough may not be left idle for longer than 18 minutes. Within that time period, it must be rolled into thin sheets and baked.

Matzah shmurah ("guarded matzah") is specially prepared from wheat carefully supervised from the time it is harvested so that it is completely dry. Grain that comes in contact with moisture starts to leaven within18 minutes. The shmurah matzah is guarded and supervised by observant Jews. *Shmurah matzah* is also called mitzvah matzah.

The three matzot The Jews of Cochin, India, mark the three matzot with lines. The Kohen matzah has two lines. The Levite matzah has three lines, and the Israelite matzah has four lines. They do not mark a matzah with one line, since only Adonai is One.

Point to the matzah and say:

1 מַצָּה זוֹ שֶׁאָנוּ אוֹכְלִים עַל־שׁוּם מָה? עַל־שׁוּם, שֶׁלֹּא

2 הִסְפִּיק בְּצֵקָם שֶׁל אֲבוֹתֵינוּ לְהַחֲמִיץ, עַד שֶׁנִּגְלָה עֲלֵיהֶם,

3 מֶלֶךְ מַלְכֵי הַמְּלָכִים הַקָּדוֹשׁ בָּרוּךְ הוּא, וּגְאָלָם. שֶׁנֶּאֱמַר:

4 וַיֹּאפוּ אֶת־הַבָּצֵק, אֲשֶׁר הוֹצִיאוּ מִמִּצְרַיִם, עֻגֹת מַצּוֹת

5 כִּי לֹא חָמֵץ. כִּי־גֹרְשׁוּ מִמִּצְרַיִם, וְלֹא יָכְלוּ לְהִתְמַהְמֵהַּ,

6 וְגַם־צֵדָה לֹא־עָשׂוּ לָהֶם:

Point to the bitter herbs and say:

7 מָרוֹר זֶה שֶׁאָנוּ אוֹכְלִים עַל־שׁוּם מָה? עַל־שׁוּם, שֶׁמָּרְרוּ

8 הַמִּצְרִים אֶת־חַיֵּי אֲבוֹתֵינוּ בְּמִצְרָיִם, שֶׁנֶּאֱמַר: וַיְמָרֲרוּ

9 אֶת־חַיֵּיהֶם בַּעֲבֹדָה קָשָׁה, בְּחֹמֶר וּבִלְבֵנִים, וּבְכָל־עֲבֹדָה

10 בַּשָּׂדֶה. אֵת כָּל־עֲבֹדָתָם, אֲשֶׁר־עָבְדוּ בָהֶם בְּפָרֶךְ:

This Matzah The Torah tells us that the Israelites took their dough before it was leavened. "Then they tied kneading troughs with the unleavened dough to their clothes upon their shoulders" (Exodus 12:34).

They made their lives bitter The Egyptian slavemasters said to the Israelites, "Each day you must complete the same amount of bricks as when you were given straw." The Israelite foremen were beaten by Pharaoh's slave masters, "Why," they asked, " have you not completed the required number of bricks?" The Israelite foremen submitted to beatings rather than force their brethren to overwork. The Midrash says that God saw the bravery of the Israelite foremen, and as a reward for their suffering they were appointed members of the Sanhedrin, Israel's highest court. In the concentration camps, the Nazis appointed Jewish foremen to control the inmates. They too were beaten and sent to the gas chambers because they refused to enforce the commands of the Nazis.

Point to the matzah and say;

<u>This Matzah</u> Why do we eat matzah on Passover? Because there was not time to add leaven to the bread, which our ancestors were baking, to rise before the Eternal freed them from slavery in Egypt. The Torah says, "And the dough which our ancestors brought out of Egypt was baked into matzah because we had no time to prepare food for the journey."

Point to the bitter herbs and say;

This Maror Why do we eat bitter herbs on Passover? Because the Egyptians made the lives of our ancestors bitter. The Torah says, "<u>They made their lives bitter </u>with hard labor <u>in cement and bricks</u> and with every kind of hard back-breaking field work."

In cement and bricks Sometimes straw is added to the mud to strengthen the mixture for making bricks. The mixture of straw, mud, and water is packed into wooden frames, forming mud bricks of the desired size and shape. The wet bricks are then placed in a sunny spot for drying. The mortar that was used to bind the bricks together was also mud. Structures made of such bricks are usually low, with thick walls and protective roofs. The dried mud is an excellent insulator, keeping the summer heat out and retaining the warmth of a furnace or a fireplace in cold weather. The fact that archaeologists have found and identified mud-brick storage buildings and other structures in Pithom attests to their durability.
In places where there is no stone or wood, people have built homes with sun-dried mud bricks. Dried mud, in this country known by its Mexican name, adobe, makes an excellent building material as long as it is protected from moisture.
In fact the oldest buildings in the United States, found in the Southwest, are adobe structures built by Indians hundreds of years ago.

בְּכָל־דּוֹר וָדוֹר חַיָּב אָדָם לִרְאוֹת אֶת־עַצְמוֹ, כְּאִלּוּ הוּא 1

יָצָא מִמִּצְרָיִם. שֶׁנֶּאֱמַר: וְהִגַּדְתָּ לְבִנְךָ בַּיּוֹם הַהוּא לֵאמֹר. 2

בַּעֲבוּר זֶה, עָשָׂה יְיָ לִי, בְּצֵאתִי מִמִּצְרָיִם: לֹא אֶת־אֲבוֹתֵינוּ 3

בִּלְבָד גָּאַל הַקָּדוֹשׁ בָּרוּךְ הוּא, אֶלָּא אַף אוֹתָנוּ גָּאַל 4

עִמָּהֶם. שֶׁנֶּאֱמַר: וְאוֹתָנוּ הוֹצִיא מִשָּׁם. לְמַעַן הָבִיא אֹתָנוּ, 5

לָתֵת לָנוּ אֶת־הָאָרֶץ, אֲשֶׁר נִשְׁבַּע לַאֲבֹתֵינוּ: 6

In every generation The essence of the Seder is not just to retell the story
of the Exodus but to turn back the clock and to act and feel the misery of
slavery. And then to sing with joy and thanksgiving at the redemption from
Egypt. At this point of the Seder, we will shortly begin the recitation of the
thanksgiving prayer, the Egyptian Hallel.

In every generation each one of us must feel and think as if we ourselves, in our own person, every one of us at this Seder, had come out of Egypt. The Torah says: "And you shall tell your child, saying: 'It is because of what the the Eternal did for me that I was saved from slavery in Egypt.'" The Eternal not only freed our ancestors, but all of us with them. The Torah says: "The Eternal freed us from slavery in Egypt, to lead us <u>to the land which was promised to our ancestors</u>."

To the land which was promised to our ancestors The land which was promised to the Children of Israel was Canaan.

At first the twelve tribes were combined into a kingdom called Israel. Later Israel split into two kingdoms. The northern kingdom of ten tribes was called Israel. The southern kingdom called itself Judea, for they were mainly descendants of Jacob's fourth son, Judah.

In the 8th century B.C.E., Assyria conquered the northern kingdom, Israel, and its people became the Ten Lost Tribes. But though the Babylonians conquered the southern kingdom in 586 B.C.E., the people of Judah have survived and are the Jewish people of today. The name Jew comes from the name Judah.

The land of Israel has also been known by many names. Some peoples called it Canaan (from Canaanites), or Palestine (from the Philistines), or Judea (from Judah). The prophets often called it Zion, which is actually the name of a hill in Jerusalem. For centuries Jews have called it Israel, the Land of Israel. Today it is known the world over as the State of Israel.

Raise the wine cup and say:

1 לְפִיכָךְ, אֲנַחְנוּ חַיָּבִים לְהוֹדוֹת, לְהַלֵּל, לְשַׁבֵּחַ, לְפָאֵר,

2 לְרוֹמֵם, לְהַדֵּר, לְבָרֵךְ, לְעַלֵּה וּלְקַלֵּס, לְמִי שֶׁעָשָׂה

3 לַאֲבוֹתֵינוּ וְלָנוּ, אֶת־כָּל־הַנִּסִּים הָאֵלּוּ. הוֹצִיאָנוּ מֵעַבְדוּת

4 לְחֵרוּת. מִיָּגוֹן לְשִׂמְחָה. וּמֵאֵבֶל לְיוֹם טוֹב. וּמֵאֲפֵלָה לְאוֹר

5 גָּדוֹל. וּמִשִּׁעְבּוּד לִגְאֻלָּה.

6 וְנֹאמַר לְפָנָיו שִׁירָה חֲדָשָׁה, הַלְלוּיָהּ:

Put down the cup and continue:
HALLEL - PSALMS OF PRAISE
Psalm 113

7 הַלְלוּיָהּ. הַלְלוּ עַבְדֵי יְיָ.   הַלְלוּ אֶת־שֵׁם יְיָ:

8 יְהִי שֵׁם יְיָ מְבֹרָךְ.   מֵעַתָּה וְעַד־עוֹלָם:

9 מִמִּזְרַח־שֶׁמֶשׁ עַד־מְבוֹאוֹ.   מְהֻלָּל שֵׁם יְיָ:

10 רָם עַל־כָּל־גּוֹיִם יְיָ.   עַל הַשָּׁמַיִם כְּבוֹדוֹ:

11 מִי כַּיְיָ אֱלֹהֵינוּ.   הַמַּגְבִּיהִי לָשָׁבֶת:

12 הַמַּשְׁפִּילִי לִרְאוֹת   בַּשָּׁמַיִם וּבָאָרֶץ:

13 מְקִימִי מֵעָפָר דָּל.   מֵאַשְׁפֹּת יָרִים אֶבְיוֹן:

14 לְהוֹשִׁיבִי עִם־נְדִיבִים   עִם נְדִיבֵי עַמּוֹ:

15 מוֹשִׁיבִי עֲקֶרֶת הַבַּיִת   אֵם־הַבָּנִים שְׂמֵחָה, הַלְלוּיָהּ:

From darkness to great light. Passover is celebrated in the spring at a time when creation awakens from the darkness of winter and begins to pulse with new life. The heavenly bodies start to shine with great intensity and spread new life and energy upon nature. Green grass covers the earth, shade and fruit trees spring to life, and the fields are carpeted with a rainbow of flowers. Creatures emerge from their underground dens, and chirping birds return from their winter homes. It was at this time of the year, in the springtime, that Adonai presented the Israelites with a soul, and a new nation was born. It was at this time that Adonai's presence was felt, and Israel was given a new life and emerged from the darkness of slavery to the great light of freedom.

Raise the wine cup and say:

It is our duty to thank the Eternal in song and prayer, to glorify the Eternal who performed all of these wonders for our ancestors and for us. The Eternal brought us out from slavery to freedom, from pain to joy, from sorrow to happiness, from darkness to great light, and from slavery to freedom. Let us sing a new song to the Eternal. Halleluyah: Praise the Eternal.

Put down the cup and continue:

HALLEL - PSALMS OF PRAISE *Psalm 113*
Halleluyah: Praise the Eternal.
> Servants of the Eternal, praise the Eternal.
> > Praise the name of the Eternal.
> Blessed the name of the Eternal from this time and forever.
> From the rising of the sun to its going down.
> > Praised be the name of the Eternal.
> Above all the nations is the Eternal.
> > The Eternal's glory is above the heavens.
> > Who looks down on the heavens and the earth?
> The Eternal raises up the poor from the dust.
> > Lifts up the poor from the ash heap
> To seat them with princes. With princes of His people.
> The Eternal makes the childless woman
> > A joyous mother of children.
> Halleluyah: Praise the Eternal.

Hallel The designation Hallel (Hymns of Praise) is usually applied to Psalms 113-118. The full title of these six psalms is the "Egyptian Hallel" because of the references to the Egyptian Exodus. At first the Hallel psalms were expressions of thanksgiving for special deliverances, but in time the sages made them binding on the three festivals: Passover, Shavuot, and Sukkot. The complete Hallel is not recited on the last six days of Passover because of the death of the pursuing Egyptians. The rabbis wisely decided that there could be no complete rejoicing if freedom was accompanied by human suffering even though it was the enemy.

Psalm 114
תְּהִלִּים קי״ד

1 בְּצֵאת יִשְׂרָאֵל מִמִּצְרָיִם. בֵּית יַעֲקֹב מֵעַם לֹעֵז: הָיְתָה

2 יְהוּדָה לְקָדְשׁוֹ. יִשְׂרָאֵל מַמְשְׁלוֹתָיו: הַיָּם רָאָה וַיָּנֹס. הַיַּרְדֵּן

3 יִסֹּב לְאָחוֹר: הֶהָרִים רָקְדוּ כְאֵילִים. גְּבָעוֹת כִּבְנֵי־צֹאן:

4 מַה־לְּךָ הַיָּם כִּי תָנוּס. הַיַּרְדֵּן תִּסֹּב לְאָחוֹר: הֶהָרִים תִּרְקְדוּ

5 כְאֵילִים. גְּבָעוֹת כִּבְנֵי־צֹאן: מִלִּפְנֵי אָדוֹן חוּלִי אָרֶץ. מִלִּפְנֵי

6 אֱלוֹהַּ יַעֲקֹב: הַהֹפְכִי הַצּוּר אֲגַם־מָיִם. חַלָּמִישׁ לְמַעְיְנוֹ־

7 מָיִם:

Psalm 114 Each letter in Hebrew has a numerical value. For example: Alef א is l, Bet ב is 2, etc. This Hebrew psalm is number. 114 קי״ד The letter Kaf ק has a value of 100. Yud י is 10, and Dalet ד is 4, making a total of 114.

When Israel left Egypt Jacob (Israel) and his family of 70 people went down to live in Egypt with his son Joseph. About four hundred and thirty years later the Children of Israel left the land of Egypt. According to the Torah, the Israelites now numbered 600,000 people. Freedom is like a contagious virus, and travels and affects all people. When the Hebrews left, many non-Jews joined the march to freedom. The Torah makes clear that some non-Jewish elements left Egypt with the Hebrews. Egyptian sources point out that tens of thousands of workers, people from many countries, labored for the Egyptian state. Also, large numbers of captives were brought to Egypt as slaves. Great building projects employed these "mixed multitudes," many of whom were no doubt eager to escape to freedom.

O Jordan, why have you stopped flowing All of God's creations reacted joyfully to the Exodus from slavery. At God's command, powerful mountains and massive hills quaked with joy. The sea and the Jordan rejoiced by creating a dry path so the Israelites could cross in safety.

Psalm 114

<u>When Israel left Egypt.</u>
    The house of Jacob was freed from foreign domination.
    Judah became the Eternal's holy place.
      Israel the Eternal's dominion.
The sea beheld and fled.
    The Jordan stopped flowing.
    The mountains skipped like rams.
      The hills like lambs.
O sea, what makes you run away,
    <u>O Jordan, why have you stopped flowing?</u>
You mountains, why do you skip like rams,
    You hills, like lambs?
Quake earth, before the Eternal,
    At the presence of the God of Jacob,
Who turned <u>the rock into a pool of water.</u>
    The firestone into a fountain of water.

The rock into a pool of water After the Israelites escaped from Egypt, they began their 40-year trek in the desert. When they reached a place called Rephidim, they began to complain to Moses because of the lack of water. The Torah tells us, "The people were tormented by thirst and they continued to grumble and criticize Moses." They said, "Why did you bring us here out of Egypt to kill us, our children, and our cattle with thirst?" Then Moses cried to the Lord, "What shall I do with this people? They are almost ready to stone me!" And the Lord said to Moses, "Go before the people and take with you some of the elders of Israel. In your hand take the rod with which you struck the Nile, and go ahead, I will be present at the rock in Horeb. You will strike the rock, and water will come pouring out of it, so that the people may drink." Moses did this in the sight of the elders of the people, and the water began to flow.

God said to Moses "The elders will be witnesses to the fact that it is because of you that water will come from the rock and that there were no springs of water hidden underneath."

The rod was used in Egypt as a means of destruction. Now God tells Moses to use it as an instrument for good.

92

Raise the cup of wine and say:

1 בָּרוּךְ אַתָּה יְיָ אֱלֹהֵינוּ מֶלֶךְ הָעוֹלָם, אֲשֶׁר גְּאָלָנוּ וְגָאַל אֶת־

2 אֲבוֹתֵינוּ מִמִּצְרַיִם, וְהִגִּיעָנוּ הַלַּיְלָה הַזֶּה, לֶאֱכָל־בּוֹ מַצָּה

3 וּמָרוֹר. כֵּן, יְיָ אֱלֹהֵינוּ וֵאלֹהֵי אֲבוֹתֵינוּ, יַגִּיעֵנוּ לְמוֹעֲדִים

4 וְלִרְגָלִים אֲחֵרִים, הַבָּאִים לִקְרָאתֵנוּ לְשָׁלוֹם, שְׂמֵחִים

5 בְּבִנְיַן עִירֶךָ, וְשָׂשִׂים בַּעֲבוֹדָתֶךָ, וְנֹאכַל שָׁם מִן הַזְּבָחִים

6 וּמִן הַפְּסָחִים, (במוצאי שבת אומרים מִן הַפְּסָחִים וּמִן

7 הַזְּבָחִים), אֲשֶׁר יַגִּיעַ דָּמָם, עַל־קִיר מִזְבַּחֲךָ לְרָצוֹן, וְנוֹדֶה

8 לְךָ שִׁיר חָדָשׁ עַל־גְּאֻלָּתֵנוּ, וְעַל־פְּדוּת נַפְשֵׁנוּ:

9 בָּרוּךְ אַתָּה יְיָ, גָּאַל יִשְׂרָאֵל:

Feasts and festivals The Shalosh Regalim are the three joyous pilgrimage festivals. These three holidays were originally agricultural in nature. Passover marked the spring barley harvest in Israel, Shavuot commemorated the summer wheat harvest, and Sukkot celebrated the autumn harvest in the Holy Land. During the three festival seasons, the Israelites would march from all four corners of the land to the Holy Temple in Jerusalem. They wanted to thank God for sending the gift of rain to water the land and the sun to warm it. The word *shalosh* means "three." The name Shalosh Regalim is derived from the custom of marching on foot. The word *regal* means "foot" *regalim* (pl) "feet".

Raise the cup of wine and say:

Blessed are You, Eternal our God, Ruler of the universe,
Who freed us and our ancestors from Egypt, and brought
us together this night to eat matzah and bitter herbs.
May the Eternal, our God and God of our ancestors,
bring us to future <u>feasts and festivals</u> in peace; and to the
rebuilding of Your city Jerusalem, and to the happiness of
Your service, so that we may partake of the ancient
offerings. We shall then offer to You a new song for our
redemption and salvation.

Blessed are you, Eternal, who redeemed Israel.

THE SECOND CUP OF WINE
*Raise your wine cup and thank the Eternal for bringing
your ancestors out of slavery.*

10 בָּרוּךְ אַתָּה יְיָ אֱלֹהֵינוּ מֶלֶךְ הָעוֹלָם, בּוֹרֵא, פְּרִי הַגָּפֶן:

Drink the second cup of wine.

WASH THE HANDS (6)   רָחְצָה
Wash the hands and say:

1 בָּרוּךְ אַתָּה יְיָ אֱלֹהֵינוּ מֶלֶךְ הָעוֹלָם, אֲשֶׁר קִדְּשָׁנוּ בְּמִצְוֹתָיו,
2 וְצִוָּנוּ עַל־נְטִילַת יָדָיִם:

THE SECOND CUP OF WINE
Raise your wine cup and thank the Eternal for bringing your ancestors out of slavery.

Blessed are You, Eternal our God, Ruler of the universe,
Creator of the fruit of the vine.
Baruch atah adonay elohey-nu melech ha-o-lam borey-p'ree ha-ga-fen.

Drink the second cup of wine.

RACHTZAH - WASH THE HANDS (6)
Wash the hands and say:

Blessed are You, Eternal our God, Ruler of the universe,
Who makes us holy with the commandments, and commanded us to wash our hands.

Baruch atah adonay elohey-nu melech ha-o-lam asher kid-sha-nu b'mits-vo-tav v'tsiva-nu al n'teelat yadayim.

MOTZI MATZAH (7) מוֹצִיא מַצָּה
Say the two blessing over the matzah:

1 בָּרוּךְ אַתָּה יְיָ אֱלֹהֵינוּ מֶלֶךְ הָעוֹלָם, הַמּוֹצִיא לֶחֶם מִן־
2 הָאָרֶץ:
3 בָּרוּךְ אַתָּה יְיָ אֱלֹהֵינוּ מֶלֶךְ הָעוֹלָם, אֲשֶׁר קִדְּשָׁנוּ בְּמִצְוֹתָיו,
4 וְצִוָּנוּ עַל־אֲכִילַת מַצָּה:

Eat the matzah.

BITTER HERBS (8) מָרוֹר
Dip bitter herbs in haroset and say:

5 בָּרוּךְ אַתָּה יְיָ אֱלֹהֵינוּ מֶלֶךְ הָעוֹלָם, אֲשֶׁר קִדְּשָׁנוּ בְּמִצְוֹתָיו,
6 וְצִוָּנוּ עַל־אֲכִילַת מָרוֹר:

Matzah In some Sephardic communities the women were the bakers of matzah, because they were the bakers throughout the year. As they baked they read psalms and sang songs. In Yemen, it was the custom for the women to bake fresh matzot each day of Passover. Among the Ashkenazim, in Europe, both men and women were allowed to bake matzot. Each person specialized in a particular process because the matzot had to be made within an 18-minute time period. One kneaded, another rolled, and a third made the holes in the matzot. A fourth person hurriedly placed the matzot into the oven.

Some matzot are baked with fruit juice or with eggs. This type of special matzah is called *matzah ashirah* (enriched matzah). Matzot ashirah may not be used at all during Passover. Plain matzah reminds us of the bread of affliction our ancestors ate in Egypt.

MOTZI MATZAH (7)
Say the two blessings over the matzah:
Blessed are you, Eternal our God, Ruler of the
universe, Who brings forth bread from the earth.

Baruch atah adonay elohey-nu melech ha-o-lam ha-motzi
lachem min ha-aretz

Blessed are you, Eternal our God, Ruler of the universe,
Who made us holy with the commandments, and
commanded us to eat the <u>matzah.</u>

Baruch atah adonay elohey-nu melech ha-o-lam asher
kid-sha-nu b'mits-vo-tav v'tsiva-nu al achilat matzah.
Eat the matzah.

MAROR - BITTER HERBS (8)
Dip bitter herbs in haroset and say:
Blessed are you, Eternal our God, Ruler of the
universe,Who made us holy with the commandments, and
commanded us to eat the bitter herbs.

Baruch atah adonay elohey-nu melech ha-o-lam asher
kid-sha-nu b'mits-vo-tav v'tsiva-nu al achilat maror
Eat the bitter herbs.

Maror The eighth step in the Seder ceremony is the eating of maror, the
bitter herbs. In this ceremony you dip the maror into the charoset and
recite a blessing. You eat maror at the Seder because it reminds us of the
pain and suffering of our people in Egypt. You eat charoset at the Seder
because it reminds us of the cement our people made when they were
slaves in Egypt.

SANDWICH OF MATZAH AND MAROR (9) כּוֹרֵךְ
Eat a sandwich of bitter herbs and matzah and say:

1 **זֵכֶר לְמִקְדָּשׁ** כְּהִלֵּל. כֵּן עָשָׂה הִלֵּל, בִּזְמַן שֶׁבֵּית הַמִּקְדָּשׁ
2 הָיָה קַיָּם. הָיָה כּוֹרֵךְ מַצָּה וּמָרוֹר וְאוֹכֵל בְּיַחַד. לְקַיֵּם מַה
3 שֶׁנֶּאֱמַר: עַל־מַצּוֹת וּמְרֹרִים יֹאכְלֻהוּ:

Korech According to Hillel, matzah, maror and the Pascal lamb were eaten together in a sandwich. Other rabbinic authorities disagree and suggest that the three foods were eaten separately. Today, we eat a matzot and maror sandwich called Korech after eating matzah and maror separately. In some communities it is customary to eat an egg dipped in salt water after the Korech ceremony. There are authorities who believe that the egg is a substitute for the *(Korban Hagigah)* Passover offering. Another reason is that the egg is a symbol of mourning and thus the egg has become a symbol of mourning for the destruction of Jerusalem. Some people believe that we dip the egg into salt water to remind ourselves of the destruction of Sodom, which tradition says took place on the night of Passover. The entire valley of Sodom, which was originally fertile, became the Dead Sea. It is here that Lot's wife ignored God's warning and looked back to see what had become of the city, and she was turned into a pillar of salt.

KORECH - SANDWICH OF MATZAH AND MAROR (9)
Eat a sandwich of bitter herbs and matzah and say:

In remembrance of the Holy Temple, we follow
<u>the practice of Hillel</u> **from Temple times: He combined
matzah and maror and ate them as a sandwich, to
observe the words of the Torah: "They shall eat it
(the Passover offering) with matzah and maror."**

Korech The ninth step in the Seder ceremony is Korech: the sandwich.
In this ceremony you make a sandwich of maror between two pieces of
matzot. No blessing is recited. You eat a sandwich of matzah and maror,
because matzah and maror together tell the story of Passover.
The lives of the Jews in Egypt were filled with maror. After the tenth
plague they left Egypt in a great hurry. The raw dough had no time to
rise and turn into bread. So our ancestors strapped the raw dough to their
backpacks and let the hot desert sun bake the dough into matzot.

The practice of Hillel Hillel was the greatest rabbi of the Second Temple
period. His wisdom and scholarship led to his appointment as nasi
(president) of the Sanhedrin. He was the founder of the school of
talmudic scholarship called Beth Hillel.
Hillel is especially remembered for having originated the golden rule.
One day a non-Jew approached him and said that he would convert to
Judaism if the rabbi could teach him the whole Torah while he was standing on one foot.
Hillel replied, "What is hateful to you, do not do to your neighbor."

THE SEDER MEAL (10) שֻׁלְחָן עוֹרֵךְ
After the meal, the afkomen is distributed
EAT THE AFIKOMEN. (11) צָפוּן
Fill the third cup of wine
GRACE AFTER THE SEDER MEAL (12) בָּרֵךְ
Psalm 126
A Pilgrim Song.

1 שִׁיר הַמַּעֲלוֹת

2 בְּשׁוּב יְיָ אֶת־שִׁיבַת צִיּוֹן הָיִינוּ כְּחֹלְמִים:

3 אָז יִמָּלֵא שְׂחוֹק פִּינוּ וּלְשׁוֹנֵנוּ רִנָּה.

4 אָז יֹאמְרוּ בַגּוֹיִם הִגְדִּיל יְיָ לַעֲשׂוֹת עִם־אֵלֶּה:

5 הִגְדִּיל יְיָ לַעֲשׂוֹת עִמָּנוּ הָיִינוּ שְׂמֵחִים:

6 שׁוּבָה יְיָ אֶת־שְׁבִיתֵנוּ כַּאֲפִיקִים בַּנֶּגֶב:

7 הַזֹּרְעִים בְּדִמְעָה בְּרִנָּה יִקְצֹרוּ:

8 הָלוֹךְ יֵלֵךְ וּבָכֹה נֹשֵׂא מֶשֶׁךְ־הַזָּרַע.

9 בֹּא־יָבֹא בְרִנָּה נֹשֵׂא אֲלֻמֹּתָיו:

The Seder Meal The tenth ceremony of the Seder is known as Shulchan Orech: mealtime. In some families the meal begins with hard-boiled eggs dipped in salt water. The eggs symbolize new growth, new life, and hope. The roasted egg on the Seder plate represents the holiday offering (Korban Haggigah) during Temple days.

Some scholars believe that the custom of eating a hard-boiled egg is based on the following idea: The more you boil an egg, the tougher it becomes. The more the Egyptians punished the Israelites, the stronger and tougher they became.

Afikomen The Torah says that the freed slaves "carried their dough before it was leavened on wood trays tied up to their clothing." In rememberance, we wrap a piece of matzah (afikomen) in a cloth as if we too were Israelites leaving Egypt. There is another reason for the afikomen.

A poor person, not knowing when he or she will eat again, will hide some food for another meal. At the Seder we play the part of the hungry person and hide a piece of matzah, for the next meal.

SHULCHAN ORECH - THE SEDER MEAL (10)
After the meal, the afikomen is distributed
TZAFUN - EAT THE AFIKOMEN. (11)
Fill the third cup of wine
BARECH - GRACE AFTER THE SEDER MEAL (12)
Psalm 126

A Pilgrim Song.

> **When the Eternal brought the exiles back to Zion**
> **We were as in a dream.**
> **Our mouth was filled with laughter,**
> **And our tongue with song.**
> **They said among the nations:**
> **"The Eternal has done great things for them."**
> **Yes, the Lord did great things for us**
> **And we are very happy.**
> **O Eternal, restore our good fortune,**
> **As dry streams that flow again.**
> **They who plant in tears shall reap in joy.**
> **Though the farmer may weep**
> **As he carries seed to the field,**
> **He will yet return with joy,**
> **Carrying the sheaves of grain.**

Grace after the Meal The Seder meal is finished and you recite a special "thank you" prayer called Birkat Hamazon. When you say the Birkat Hamazon, you are thanking God for the food that you have eaten. You ask God to keep on blessing our parents, our relatives, our friends, and the whole world, with food and with peace.

Tzafun The eleventh ceremony of the Seder is known as Tzafun, which means "hidden." At the end of the meal, the leader searches for the hidden afikomen. Whoever returns it gets a reward.

Nothing is eaten after the afikomen, so that matzah, the bread of freedom, is the last food tasted. We have an afikomen at the Seder because when you are a slave nobody is kind to you and gives you presents. The Seder is your "freedom birthday party." And what's a birthday party without presents?

When ten or more adults are present, the words in parentheses
are added.

1 The leader: רַבּוֹתַי נְבָרֵךְ:

2 All assembled: יְהִי שֵׁם יְיָ מְבֹרָךְ מֵעַתָּה וְעַד עוֹלָם:

3 The leader: בִּרְשׁוּת מָרָנָן וְרַבָּנָן וְרַבּוֹתַי, נְבָרֵךְ (אֱלֹהֵינוּ)

4 שֶׁאָכַלְנוּ מִשֶּׁלּוֹ:

5 All assembled: בָּרוּךְ (אֱלֹהֵינוּ) שֶׁאָכַלְנוּ מִשֶּׁלּוֹ וּבְטוּבוֹ חָיִינוּ:

6 בָּרוּךְ הוּא וּבָרוּךְ שְׁמוֹ:

7 בָּרוּךְ אַתָּה יְיָ אֱלֹהֵינוּ מֶלֶךְ הָעוֹלָם, הַזָּן אֶת־הָעוֹלָם כֻּלּוֹ,

8 בְּטוּבוֹ, בְּחֵן בְּחֶסֶד וּבְרַחֲמִים, הוּא נוֹתֵן לֶחֶם לְכָל־בָּשָׂר

9 כִּי לְעוֹלָם חַסְדּוֹ. וּבְטוּבוֹ הַגָּדוֹל, תָּמִיד לֹא־חָסַר לָנוּ,

10 וְאַל־יֶחְסַר לָנוּ מָזוֹן לְעוֹלָם וָעֶד. בַּעֲבוּר שְׁמוֹ הַגָּדוֹל,

11 כִּי הוּא אֵל זָן וּמְפַרְנֵס לַכֹּל וּמֵטִיב לַכֹּל וּמֵכִין מָזוֹן

12 לְכָל־בְּרִיּוֹתָיו אֲשֶׁר בָּרָא: בָּרוּךְ אַתָּה יְיָ, הַזָּן אֶת־הַכֹּל:

Barech The twelfth ceremony of the Seder is known as Barech. After the afkomen the Seder resumes with the "thank you" prayer, Birkat Hamazon.

With the permission The Seder leader must, invite a guest to lead the Grace, who says "Let us say Grace." After inviting the guests and their response, the leader asks permission to continue with the Grace.
The Grace after meals consist of four ancient blessings, each with a special theme which reflects Israel's spiritual and national growth.

continued on page 103

When ten or more adults are present, the words in parentheses are added.

The Leader: Let us say Grace.

All assembled: May the name of the Lord be blessed from this time forth and forever.

Leader: <u>With the permission</u> of all present, let us bless Him (our God) whose food we have eaten.

All assembled: Blessed be the Eternal (our God) Whose food we have eaten and in Whose goodness we live.

Leader repeats: Blessed be the Eternal (our God) Whose food we

Blessed is the Eternal and Blessed is the Holy Name.
Blessed are You, O Eternal our God, Ruler of all the world, Who feeds the entire world with goodness, with grace, with kindness and with mercy. You give food to all people, for Your kindness lasts forever. Because of Your great goodness, we have never lacked food. You provide food for all the creatures You have created.
Blessed are You, O Eternal, Who gives food to everyone.

---

1. The first benediction is the oldest and thanks God for providing sustenance for every creature in the world.
2. The second blessing thanks God for the land of Israel and the redemption from Egypt. Throughout their 4,000 years of history no matter where they lived, Jews have never have given up their claim to the land of Israel.
The modern-day State of Israel is a symbol of their prayers, hopes, and faith that the biblical prophecy of the Return to Zion has come to fruition.
3. The third benediction continues to thank God for Israel and Jerusalem and asks for security and happiness and for the elimination of poverty. It ends with a plea for the rebuilding of Jerusalem, the spiritual center of the Jewish people.
4. The fourth and last benediction is called the Blessing of Goodness. We thank God for all the goodness that has been bestowed upon the Jewish people.

1 **נוֹדֶה לְךָ** יְיָ אֱלֹהֵינוּ עַל שֶׁהִנְחַלְתָּ לַאֲבוֹתֵינוּ, אֶרֶץ חֶמְדָּה

2 טוֹבָה וּרְחָבָה. וְעַל שֶׁהוֹצֵאתָנוּ, יְיָ אֱלֹהֵינוּ, מֵאֶרֶץ מִצְרַיִם,

3 וּפְדִיתָנוּ מִבֵּית עֲבָדִים. וְעַל בְּרִיתְךָ שֶׁחָתַמְתָּ בִּבְשָׂרֵנוּ,

4 וְעַל תּוֹרָתְךָ שֶׁלִּמַּדְתָּנוּ, וְעַל חֻקֶּיךָ שֶׁהוֹדַעְתָּנוּ, וְעַל חַיִּים

5 חֵן וָחֶסֶד שֶׁחוֹנַנְתָּנוּ, וְעַל אֲכִילַת מָזוֹן שָׁאַתָּה זָן וּמְפַרְנֵס

6 אוֹתָנוּ תָּמִיד, בְּכָל־יוֹם וּבְכָל־עֵת וּבְכָל־שָׁעָה:

7 **וְעַל הַכֹּל** יְיָ אֱלֹהֵינוּ, אֲנַחְנוּ מוֹדִים לָךְ, וּמְבָרְכִים אוֹתָךְ,

8 יִתְבָּרַךְ שִׁמְךָ, בְּפִי כָּל־חַי, תָּמִיד לְעוֹלָם וָעֶד. כַּכָּתוּב,

9 וְאָכַלְתָּ וְשָׂבָעְתָּ, וּבֵרַכְתָּ אֶת־יְיָ אֱלֹהֶיךָ, עַל־הָאָרֶץ הַטֹּבָה

10 אֲשֶׁר־נָתַן לָךְ: בָּרוּךְ אַתָּה יְיָ, עַל הָאָרֶץ וְעַל הַמָּזוֹן:

For the food You are always providing us God provides food for all creatures. In the ancient Hebrew state, the poor were assured of a living by the rights which the Torah gave them in the harvest. These rights were five in number.

1. The poor had the right to any crops that grew in the corners of the field. This was known as *Peah* (Corner).

2. They had the right to crops dropped on the ground. This was called *Leket* (gleanings).

3. They had the right to isolated grapes on the vine. This was called P*eret*

4. They had the right to grapes that were not perfect. This was called *Olelot* (Young Clusters).

5. They had the right to sheaves that were forgotten by the farmer. This was called *Shikchah* (Forgetfulness).

All these parts of the harvest belonged to the poor. The farmer was not allowed to gather them, and all needy people were entitled to them. There was also a special tax known as the Poor Tithe. Twice in seven years the Jewish farmer had to set aside one tenth of his harvest for distribution to the needy.

O Eternal, we thank You, because You gave our ancestors a land that is pleasant, goodly, and spacious, and because You brought our ancestors forth from a land of slavery. We also thank You <u>for Your Torah,</u> for the laws You made known to us, for the life, grace, and kindness You have granted us, and <u>for the food You are always providing us</u> every day, every season, every hour.

O Eternal, for all this, we thank and bless You. May Your name be blessed forever and ever by all that live, just as it is written in the Torah: "Eat and be satisfied, and then bless the Eternal your God for the good land given to you." O Eternal, blessed are You, for the land and for the food You have given us.

For Your Torah The Midrash tells us that God first offered the Torah to other nations around the world, but they all refused it. God asked the first nation, "Will you accept and obey the laws and the rules of the Torah?" "What does it say?" they asked. It says "You shall not kill," answered God. "Oh, no!" they replied angrily. "We live by war and by killing, and we cannot accept your Torah."
Then the Lord approached another nation and asked them to accept the Torah. They too asked, "What does this Torah of yours say?" It says, "Honor your father and your mother." "Definitely not," replied the people, "we throw out and reject our parents when they become poor, old, and useless."
God continued asking all the nations of the world, and they all found something in the Torah that they did not like. Last, God approached Israel and asked them. They replied without hesitation and in one loud voice, "All that the Lord has spoken we will do."

1   **רַחֶם־נָא** יְיָ אֱלֹהֵינוּ, עַל יִשְׂרָאֵל עַמֶּךָ, וְעַל יְרוּשָׁלַיִם עִירֶךָ,

2   וְעַל צִיּוֹן מִשְׁכַּן כְּבוֹדֶךָ, וְעַל מַלְכוּת בֵּית דָּוִד מְשִׁיחֶךָ,

3   וְעַל הַבַּיִת הַגָּדוֹל וְהַקָּדוֹשׁ שֶׁנִּקְרָא שִׁמְךָ עָלָיו.

4   אֱלֹהֵינוּ, אָבִינוּ, רְעֵנוּ, זוּנֵנוּ, פַּרְנְסֵנוּ, וְכַלְכְּלֵנוּ, וְהַרְוִיחֵנוּ,

5   וְהַרְוַח־לָנוּ יְיָ אֱלֹהֵינוּ מְהֵרָה מִכָּל־צָרוֹתֵינוּ. וְנָא, אַל־

6   תַּצְרִיכֵנוּ יְיָ אֱלֹהֵינוּ לֹא לִידֵי מַתְּנַת בָּשָׂר וָדָם, וְלֹא לִידֵי

7   הַלְוָאָתָם, כִּי אִם לְיָדְךָ הַמְּלֵאָה, הַפְּתוּחָה, הַקְּדוֹשָׁה

8   וְהָרְחָבָה, שֶׁלֹּא נֵבוֹשׁ וְלֹא נִכָּלֵם לְעוֹלָם וָעֶד:

On the Sabbath the following is said:

9   **רְצֵה וְהַחֲלִיצֵנוּ** יְיָ אֱלֹהֵינוּ, **בְּמִצְוֹתֶיךָ**, וּבְמִצְוַת יוֹם הַשְּׁבִיעִי

10   הַשַּׁבָּת הַגָּדוֹל וְהַקָּדוֹשׁ הַזֶּה. כִּי יוֹם זֶה, גָּדוֹל וְקָדוֹשׁ

11   הוּא לְפָנֶיךָ, לִשְׁבָּת־בּוֹ וְלָנוּחַ בּוֹ, בְּאַהֲבָה, כְּמִצְוַת רְצוֹנֶךָ.

12   וּבִרְצוֹנְךָ הָנִיחַ לָנוּ יְיָ אֱלֹהֵינוּ, שֶׁלֹּא תְהֵא צָרָה וְיָגוֹן

13   וַאֲנָחָה, בְּיוֹם מְנוּחָתֵנוּ. וְהַרְאֵנוּ, יְיָ אֱלֹהֵינוּ, בְּנֶחָמַת צִיּוֹן

14   עִירֶךָ, וּבְבִנְיַן יְרוּשָׁלַיִם עִיר קָדְשֶׁךָ, כִּי אַתָּה הוּא, בַּעַל

15   הַיְשׁוּעוֹת, וּבַעַל הַנֶּחָמוֹת:

Jerusalem Jerusalem is located in the heart of Israel, high in the Judean mountains. It has been called a Sacred City, the Soul of Israel, City of David, Zion, and the Center of the Universe. Jerusalem means "City of Peace." King David captured the city and made it the capital of Israel. Three thousand years later, David Ben-Gurion did the same thing when Israel was re-established. David's son, King Solomon, built the Holy Temple there and dedicated it to God's worship.

The Great Sabbath The Sabbath preceding the festival of Passover is designated as the Great Sabbath (Shabbat Hagadol) in commemoration of the great miracle that occurred on the Sabbath preceding the Exodus from Egypt. It is based on the tradition that when God ordered the Israelites to prepare lambs on the tenth of Nisan for the paschal offering, the Egyptians were paralyzed with fear and could not prevent them from doing so, even though the lamb was an Egyptian deity.

Show mercy, O Lord our God, to Israel, Your people, _Jerusalem,_ Your City, Zion in which Your glory rules, the kingdom of the house of David, and the noble and sacred house that bears Your name, O God.

O Eternal, feed and support us, and relieve us of our troubles. We pray to You, O God, never to leave us in need of help and gifts, and but let us rely only upon Your helping hand, which is always full and open. Thus may we never feel disgrace at any time or place.

On the Sabbath the following is said:

O'Eternal gives us rest through Your commandments, especially that of the Great Sabbath, the day that is so great and sacred. May we rest on the Sabbath, in loving harmony with Your will. Grant us peace without grief or sorrow. O God, may we see the rebuilding of Your holy city Jerusalem. For You are the Eternal Lord, Who will always give us deliverance and consolation.

O Eternal, feed and support us Among the many blessings we recite, the only ones the Torah specifically requires are those that we say after we eat. The Torah says, "When you have eaten and are satisfied, you shall bless Adonai your God for the good land He has given you" Deuteronomy 8:10. This biblical commandment is fulfilled by reciting three blessings: one for the food, one for the land of Israel, and one for Jerusalem. These blessings are called Birkat Hamazon (Grace after Meals). Moses was concerned that the Israelites, after a satisfying meal, would forget to thank Adonai. In Deuteronomy 8:11-18, Moses warns the Israelites, "Take care lest you forget the Lord your God and fail to keep the commandments, lest when you eat and be sated, and build fine houses to live in, and your herds and your flocks multiply, and your silver and gold increase, and everything you own prospers, beware lest your heart grow haughty and you then forget the Lord your God, and you say to yourselves, 'My own power and the might of my own hand have won this wealth for me.' Remember that it is the Lord your God who gives you the power to acquire wealth."

1 אֱלֹהֵינוּ וֵאלֹהֵי אֲבוֹתֵינוּ, יַעֲלֶה וְיָבֹא, וְיַגִּיעַ, וְיֵרָאֶה, וְיֵרָצֶה,

2 וְיִשָּׁמַע, וְיִפָּקֵד, וְיִזָּכֵר, זִכְרוֹנֵנוּ וּפִקְדוֹנֵנוּ, וְזִכְרוֹן אֲבוֹתֵינוּ,

3 וְזִכְרוֹן מָשִׁיחַ בֶּן־דָּוִד עַבְדֶּךָ, וְזִכְרוֹן יְרוּשָׁלַיִם עִיר קָדְשֶׁךָ,

4 וְזִכְרוֹן כָּל־עַמְּךָ בֵּית יִשְׂרָאֵל, לְפָנֶיךָ. לִפְלֵיטָה, לְטוֹבָה,

5 לְחֵן וּלְחֶסֶד וּלְרַחֲמִים, לְחַיִּים וּלְשָׁלוֹם, בְּיוֹם חַג הַמַּצּוֹת

6 הַזֶּה. זָכְרֵנוּ יְיָ אֱלֹהֵינוּ, בּוֹ לְטוֹבָה, וּפָקְדֵנוּ בוֹ לִבְרָכָה,

7 וְהוֹשִׁיעֵנוּ בוֹ לְחַיִּים טוֹבִים. וּבִדְבַר יְשׁוּעָה וְרַחֲמִים, חוּס

8 וְחָנֵּנוּ, וְרַחֵם עָלֵינוּ וְהוֹשִׁיעֵנוּ, כִּי אֵלֶיךָ עֵינֵינוּ, כִּי אֵל מֶלֶךְ

9 חַנּוּן וְרַחוּם אָתָּה:

Ya'aleh V'yavo Some commentators believe that the Ya'aleh V'yavoh prayer describes the bringing of the bikkurim offerings to the altar in the Holy Temple. As the pilgrims with their bikkurim approached the altar, a Kohen (priest) choreographed the approach by intoning these eight words. which directed the pilgrims:

1. Ya'aleh   - Ascend   - Take one step toward the altar.

2. Yavo   - Come   - Come forward and take another step.

3. Yage'ah   - Reach   - Reach the altar by taking a third step.

4. Yera'eh   - Appear   - Appear before the Kohen and show him the basket of bikkurim.

5. Yeratzeh   - Accept   - Acceptance of the bikkurim by the Kohen.

6. Yeshemah - Heard   - The declaration of the pilgrim donating the bikkurim is heard by the priest.

7. Yepaked   - Recorded - The Kohen records the donation of the bikkurim.

8. Yizaher   - Remember - The pilgrim prays that the Eternal will remember and reward him with good harvests in the coming year.

Eternal, God of our ancestors, <u>may we ascend, came forward,</u>
<u>reach, appear, be accepted, be heard, be recorded, and may</u>
<u>You remember us</u> with favor, and may You also remember with
favor our ancestors,

Messiah the son of David, Your servant, Jerusalem Your
holy city, and all Your people, Israel, bringing us
security and well-being, grace, kindness, and mercy, life
and peace on this day. Keep us in Your thoughts on this
day, O Eternal, to bring us well-being, blessing, and long
life. Remember Your promise to protect us; be gracious
and merciful to us. For our eyes ever turn to You, as we
know You to be a kind and merciful Ruler.

Messiah Messiah, *Mashiach* in Hebrew, is the biblical word referring
to kings who have been anointed by receiving divine approval. After the
exile the prophetic vision of the ingathering of Israel under a Messiah, a
leader of Davidic descent who would be God's anointed, entered Jewish
religious thought.
The belief in a Messiah grew even stronger after the destruction of
the Second Temple in 70 C.E.
In 131 C.E. the saintly Rabbi Akiva publicly announced that Bar Kochba,
the military leader of the short-lived second revolt against Rome, was the
Messiah. Maimonides, in his letter to the Jews of Yemen in the
12th century, glowingly restated his belief in the messianic doctrine and
even included the Messiah in his Thirteen Articles of Faith.
Over the centuries, Jews suffered from numerous pseudo-messiahs, especially in turbulent times. In 1147, David Alroy appeared in Mesopotamia.
Abraham Abulafia was active in Sicily in the 13th century, Solomon
Molcho in 1500, and Shabbati Tzvi in 1648.

1 **וּבְנֵה יְרוּשָׁלַיִם** עִיר הַקֹּדֶשׁ, בִּמְהֵרָה בְיָמֵינוּ: בָּרוּךְ אַתָּה יְיָ,

2 בּוֹנֵה בְרַחֲמָיו יְרוּשָׁלָיִם. אָמֵן:

3 **בָּרוּךְ אַתָּה** יְיָ אֱלֹהֵינוּ מֶלֶךְ הָעוֹלָם, הָאֵל אָבִינוּ, מַלְכֵּנוּ,

4 אַדִּירֵנוּ, בּוֹרְאֵנוּ, גּוֹאֲלֵנוּ, יוֹצְרֵנוּ, קְדוֹשֵׁנוּ, קְדוֹשׁ יַעֲקֹב.

5 רוֹעֵנוּ רֹעֵה יִשְׂרָאֵל. הַמֶּלֶךְ הַטּוֹב, וְהַמֵּטִיב לַכֹּל, שֶׁבְּכָל-

6 יוֹם וָיוֹם הוּא הֵטִיב, הוּא מֵטִיב, הוּא יֵיטִיב לָנוּ: הוּא

7 גְמָלָנוּ. הוּא גוֹמְלֵנוּ. הוּא יִגְמְלֵנוּ לָעַד. לְחֵן וּלְחֶסֶד,

8 וּלְרַחֲמִים וּלְרֶוַח. הַצָּלָה וְהַצְלָחָה. בְּרָכָה וִישׁוּעָה. נֶחָמָה,

9 פַּרְנָסָה וְכַלְכָּלָה. וְרַחֲמִים, וְחַיִּים וְשָׁלוֹם, וְכָל-טוֹב, וּמִכָּל-

10 טוּב לְעוֹלָם אַל-יְחַסְּרֵנוּ:

11 **הָרַחֲמָן**, הוּא יִמְלֹךְ עָלֵינוּ לְעוֹלָם וָעֶד:

12 **הָרַחֲמָן**, הוּא יִתְבָּרַךְ בַּשָּׁמַיִם וּבָאָרֶץ:

13 **הָרַחֲמָן**, הוּא יִשְׁתַּבַּח לְדוֹר דּוֹרִים, וְיִתְפָּאַר בָּנוּ לָעַד

14 וּלְנֵצַח נְצָחִים, וְיִתְהַדַּר בָּנוּ לָעַד וּלְעוֹלְמֵי עוֹלָמִים:

15 **הָרַחֲמָן**, הוּא יְפַרְנְסֵנוּ בְּכָבוֹד:

16 **הָרַחֲמָן**, הוּא יִשְׁבֹּר עֻלֵּנוּ מֵעַל צַוָּארֵנוּ, וְהוּא יוֹלִיכֵנוּ

17 קוֹמְמִיּוּת לְאַרְצֵנוּ:

18 **הָרַחֲמָן**, הוּא יִשְׁלַח לָנוּ, בְּרָכָה מְרֻבָּה בַּבַּיִת הַזֶּה, וְעַל

19 שֻׁלְחָן זֶה שֶׁאָכַלְנוּ עָלָיו:

We pray that you will rebuild Jerusalem The greatest things that ever happened in Jewish history took place in Jerusalem. King Solomon built the Holy Temple in Jerusalem. Great Jewish kings ruled in Jerusalem. Many miracles happened in Jerusalem. Three times a year, on Sukkot, Pesach, and Shavuot, Jewish farmers brought sacrifices to the Holy Temple in Jerusalem. So holy is Jerusalem that we recite our prayers facing Jerusalem, to our east.

We pray that You will rebuild Jerusalem, the holy city, soon, in our time. **Rebuild Jerusalem,** the holy city, in our days. Blessed are You, O Lord, Who in mercy will rebuild Jerusalem. Amen

Blessed are You, Eternal our God, God of all the world, our Creator, our Shepherd, who was worshipped by our ancestor Jacob, for having dealt kindly with us in the days past, for treating us today with kindness, and for the goodness You will yet show to us, in former days, in this day, and in days to come. You are the giver of all things good, granting us love and kindness and mercy and prosperity and blessing and consolation and support and a peaceful life. May we never lack of the good things granted by the Eternal.
May the Merciful One rule over us forever.
May the Merciful One be blessed in heaven and on earth.
May the Merciful One be praised throughout all generations.
May the Merciful One grant that we support ourselves in dignity.
May the Merciful One remove the oppressor's yoke from our neck and lead us proudly to our own land
May the Merciful One send blessings upon this house and upon this table from which we have eaten.

Rebuild Jerusalem There were two Temples in Jerusalem. The First Temple was built by King Solomon around 950 B.C.E. Four hundred years later in 586 B.C.E., Solomon's Temple was destroyed by the Babylonians on the 9th day of Av.
The Second Temple was built around 515 B.C.E. by the returning exiles from Babylon under the leadership of Ezra and Nehemiah. It was a small, unimposing structure but served the tiny nation as a sanctuary.
Three hundred years later, in 55 B.C.E., King Herod began enlarging and rebuilding it into a magnificent structure. It was finished in 2 C.E., several years after his death. Again on the 9th day of Av, in 70 C.E., the Second Temple was destroyed by the Romans. Hundreds of years later, the Muslims captured Jerusalem and built two mosques on the site of the ancient Jewish Temple: Al Aksa and the Dome of the Rock. These two structures are a severe problem for the modern State of Israel.
Today we remember the destruction of the two Temples on the sad holiday of Tisha B'av-the 9th day of Av.

112

1 הָרַחֲמָן, הוּא יִשְׁלַח לָנוּ, אֶת־אֵלִיָּהוּ הַנָּבִיא זָכוּר לַטּוֹב

2 וִיבַשֶּׂר־לָנוּ בְּשׂוֹרוֹת טוֹבוֹת יְשׁוּעוֹת וְנֶחָמוֹת:

3 הָרַחֲמָן, הוּא יְבָרֵךְ (אֶת־אָבִי מוֹרִי בַּעַל הַבַּיִת הַזֶּה, וְאֶת־אִמִּי

4 מוֹרָתִי, בַּעֲלַת הַבַּיִת הַזֶּה.) (אוֹתִי וְאֶת אִשְׁתִּי וְאֶת זַרְעִי

5 וְאֶת־כָּל־אֲשֶׁר לִי.)

6 אוֹתָם וְאֶת־בֵּיתָם, וְאֶת־זַרְעָם וְאֶת־כָּל־אֲשֶׁר לָהֶם. אוֹתָנוּ

7 וְאֶת־כָּל־אֲשֶׁר לָנוּ, כְּמוֹ שֶׁנִּתְבָּרְכוּ אֲבוֹתֵינוּ, אַבְרָהָם,

8 יִצְחָק וְיַעֲקֹב, בַּכֹּל, מִכֹּל, כֹּל. כֵּן יְבָרֵךְ אוֹתָנוּ, כֻּלָּנוּ יַחַד,

9 בִּבְרָכָה שְׁלֵמָה. וְנֹאמַר אָמֵן:

10 בַּמָּרוֹם יְלַמְּדוּ עֲלֵיהֶם וְעָלֵינוּ זְכוּת, שֶׁתְּהֵא לְמִשְׁמֶרֶת

11 שָׁלוֹם, וְנִשָּׂא בְרָכָה מֵאֵת יְיָ, וּצְדָקָה מֵאֱלֹהֵי יִשְׁעֵנוּ.

12 וְנִמְצָא חֵן וְשֵׂכֶל טוֹב בְּעֵינֵי אֱלֹהִים וְאָדָם:

Elijah Elijah the Tishbi prophesied in the 9th century B.C.E. during the reigns of Ahab and Ahaziah. His prophecies against idol worship and usury angered the royal court and he was forced to flee. Elijah was greatly loved by the people of Israel. Stories of his compassion and his helpfulness to the poor and the sick echoed throughout the land. In time, because of his deeds, he became a symbol of redemption and hope. Elijah occupies an important place in Jewish lore. According to the Bible, Elijah did not die but ascended to heaven in a fiery chariot. In later literature, Elijah is pictured as the harbinger of the Messiah. At the Seder table a special goblet is filled with wine for Elijah the prophet in the symbolic hope that he will bring health and prosperity to the celebrants. In our religious literature he is believed to appear and come to the aid of Jewish communities and individuals who are in distress. During circumcision ceremonies a symbolic seat called the Chair of Elijah is set aside for his coming and his blessing. In Europe chairs specially made for Elijah are to be found in many synagogues.

The prophet Elijah When we open the door for Elijah, we must also open and make a place for every Jew who wishes to regain their lost heritage.

May the Merciful One send to us <u>the prophet Elijah</u>, of blessed memory, bearing good tidings of deliverance and comfort.

May the Merciful One bless this house and all assembled here, us and all that is ours, just as our ancestors, Abraham, Isaac, and Jacob, Sarah, Rebecca, Leah, and Rachel, were blessed with every manner of blessing. May the Eternal bless all of us together with a perfect blessing, and let us say, Amen.

On high, may there be invoked for them and for us such merit as shall secure enduring peace. Then shall we receive a blessing from the Eternal and <u>righteousness</u> from the God of our salvation. And may we find grace and favor in the eyes of God and man.

The following paragraph is said on the Sabbath:

May the Merciful One grant us a day that shall be filled with Sabbath peace and rest in life everlasting.

Righteousness Tzedakah, acts of righteousness are so important a part of Jewish life that the very term "righteousness" (tzedakah) designates the giving of charitable contributions. People make tzedakah donations to a synagogue or temple to mark special occasions. They give extra tzedakah before Passover to help the needy buy matzot and other Passover foods. Jews keep tzedakah boxes in their homes, and many put money in the box before lighting Sabbath candles each Friday night. In the Middle Ages, the great scholar Maimonides put the Jewish ideas about how to give charity into a simple code called the Ladder of Tzedakah. It tells us the eight degrees of giving charity and explains the best ways to give tzedakah. Eight degrees of charity, starting with the most important.
1. Helping someone to help himself.
2. Giving anonymously to an unknown person.
3. Giving anonymously to a person you know is in need.
4. Giving without knowing who will get the gift.
5. Giving without being asked.
6. Giving after being asked.
7. Giving less than one can afford, but giving willingly.
8. Giving unwillingly.
The special Passover tzedakah fund is called Ma'ot Chittim, "Wheat Money." The fund is specially used to help Jews celebrate Passover in dignity.

The following paragraph is said on the Sabbath:

1 הָרַחֲמָן, הוּא יַנְחִילֵנוּ יוֹם שֶׁכֻּלּוֹ שַׁבָּת וּמְנוּחָה, לְחַיֵּי

2 הָעוֹלָמִים:

3 הָרַחֲמָן, הוּא יַנְחִילֵנוּ יוֹם שֶׁכֻּלּוֹ טוֹב:

4 הָרַחֲמָן, הוּא יְזַכֵּנוּ לִימוֹת הַמָּשִׁיחַ וּלְחַיֵּי הָעוֹלָם הַבָּא.

5 מִגְדּוֹל יְשׁוּעוֹת מַלְכּוֹ, וְעֹשֶׂה חֶסֶד לִמְשִׁיחוֹ, לְדָוִד וּלְזַרְעוֹ

6 עַד עוֹלָם. עֹשֶׂה שָׁלוֹם בִּמְרוֹמָיו, הוּא יַעֲשֶׂה שָׁלוֹם, עָלֵינוּ

7 וְעַל כָּל יִשְׂרָאֵל, וְאִמְרוּ אָמֵן:

8 יְראוּ אֶת־יְיָ קְדֹשָׁיו, כִּי אֵין מַחְסוֹר לִירֵאָיו: כְּפִירִים רָשׁוּ

9 וְרָעֵבוּ, וְדֹרְשֵׁי יְיָ לֹא־יַחְסְרוּ כָל־טוֹב: הוֹדוּ לַיְיָ כִּי טוֹב,

10 כִּי לְעוֹלָם חַסְדּוֹ: פּוֹתֵחַ אֶת־יָדֶךָ, וּמַשְׂבִּיעַ לְכָל־חַי רָצוֹן:

11 בָּרוּךְ הַגֶּבֶר אֲשֶׁר יִבְטַח בַּיְיָ, וְהָיָה יְיָ מִבְטַחוֹ: נַעַר הָיִיתִי,

12 גַּם זָקַנְתִּי, וְלֹא רָאִיתִי צַדִּיק נֶעֱזָב, וְזַרְעוֹ מְבַקֶּשׁ־לָחֶם: יְיָ

13 עֹז לְעַמּוֹ יִתֵּן, יְיָ יְבָרֵךְ אֶת־עַמּוֹ בַשָּׁלוֹם:

David, the second king of Israel (ca. 1000-960 B.C.E.), as a young boy killed the Philistine giant Goliath. At the age of 25 he became the armor-bearer to King Saul, and because of his military skills was rewarded by marrying Michel, Saul's daughter. After Saul and his three sons were killed at the battle of Mount Gilboa, David was crowned king. In the eighth year of his reign, David captured the Jebusite stronghold of Jerusalem and made it the capital of Israel. During his reign he defeated the nations of Aram, Philistia, Edom, and Moab and extended the frontier of Israel to include more territory than at any other time in Jewish history. Internally he aggressively organized the national administration and began preparations for building a central temple to house the Holy Ark. Under his leadership Israel became a thriving nation to which numerous monarchs paid homage. When David died, his son Solomon inherited the reins of government and built the First Temple.

continued on page 115

The following paragraph is said on the Sabbath:
May the Merciful One grant us a day that shall be all
    Sabbath and rest in life everlasting.

May the Merciful One grant us a day that shall be all good.

May the Merciful One make us worthy of the days of the
    Messiah and life in the world to come.
    "He is a tower of salvation to His king, and shows
    kindness to His anointed one, to <u>David</u> and his descen
    dants forever." May He Who makes peace in the heavenly
    spheres, grant peace to us, and to all Israel, and let us say,
    Amen.

Honor the Eternal,
    you who consider yourselves holy ones.
    Those who honor the Eternal will not suffer hunger,
    but even the mighty lion must often suffer hunger;
    But who seeks the Eternal will never lack what is good.
    Give thanks to the Eternal, for God is good.
    His kindness endures forever.
    Eternal, You open Your hand, O Eternal,
    and in favor supply living beings with all they need.
    Blessed is the person who trusts the Eternal.
    People have been young and grown old;
    But in all that time they have not seen people
    forsaken, or their children hungry for bread.
    For the Eternal gives us strength.
    He blesses us with peace.

In addition to his military and political skills, David is also accredited with composing Tehillim, the Book of Psalms. In the course of time, David became a religious symbol and the Jewish messianic hope was attached to his descendants.

As David lay dying, he instructed his son Solomon to keep God's laws as recorded in the Torah, "then your line on the throne of Israel will never end."

THE THIRD CUP OF WINE
*All together, raise your cups and celebrate the
holy joy of freedom with the wine blessing:*

1 בָּרוּךְ אַתָּה יְיָ אֱלֹהֵינוּ מֶלֶךְ הָעוֹלָם, בּוֹרֵא, פְּרִי הַגָּפֶן:

*Drink the third cup of wine. Fill the fourth cup of wine
and open the door for Elijah the Prophet. All rise.*

2 שְׁפֹךְ חֲמָתְךָ אֶל־הַגּוֹיִם אֲשֶׁר לֹא־יְדָעוּךָ,

3 וְעַל־מַמְלָכוֹת אֲשֶׁר בְּשִׁמְךָ לֹא קָרָאוּ:

4 כִּי אָכַל אֶת־יַעֲקֹב וְאֶת־נָוֵהוּ הֵשַׁמּוּ:

5 שְׁפָךְ־עֲלֵיהֶם זַעְמֶךָ וַחֲרוֹן אַפְּךָ יַשִּׂיגֵם:

6 תִּרְדֹּף בְּאַף וְתַשְׁמִידֵם, מִתַּחַת שְׁמֵי יְיָ:

Close the door. All are seated.

The fruit of the vine. The third cup of wine is for Adonai's promise to
the Children of Israel, "and I will redeem you with outstretched hands
and great judgment" (Exodus 6:6).

For they have destroyed Jacob The blood libel is the claim that Jews
kill non-Jewish children and use their blood for Passover and other
religious rituals. The blood libel led to pogroms and massacres of Jews in
the Middle Ages and even in early modern times.
Starting in the 17th century, blood libel cases were especially prevalent in
Russia and Poland. Many were incited by the church because of resent-
ment of the Jews' refusal to accept Christianity. When economic conditions deteriorated, the blood libel cases increased.
In recent times the Nazis used the blood libel for anti-Jewish propaganda.
They initiated blood libel trials in territories they controlled.

Pour out Your anger The ancient mystics taught that there is a constant
back-and-forth exchange between Adonai and the world. When the
upward flow is filled by deeds of loving-kindness (tzedekah), then there is
a downward flow of blessings and grace upon the world. However, when
the upward flow of human behavior is filled with sinful acts, the
downward flow is negative.

THE THIRD CUP OF WINE

All together, raise your cups and celebrate the holy joy of freedom with the wine blessing:

Blessed are You, Eternal our God, Ruler of the universe, Creator of <u>the fruit of the vine.</u>

Baruch atah adonay elohey-nu melech ha-o-lam borey-p'ree ha-ga-fen.

Drink the third cup of wine. Fill the fourth cup of wine and open the door for Elijah the Prophet. All rise.

<u>Pour out your anger</u> **upon the people that do not accept You, and upon the continents that do not call Your name; <u>for they have destroyed Jacob</u> and laid waste to his dwelling. Pour out Your anger upon them and let Your fury overtake them. Pursue them in anger and destroy them from under Your heavens.** *Close the door. All are seated.*

Elijah There is a covenant between God and humanity, and the actions of humans affect the redemption of the world and the coming of the Messiah. Judaism believes that Elijah and the Messianic Age are yet to come, and our acts of loving kindness, compassion, and moral deeds can bring about a world worthy of redemption.

Elijah the Prophet During the first part of the Seder, the Israelites escaped from slavery in Egypt to freedom. Now it is for us to open the door for Elijah the Prophet and usher in the time of redemption for all people.

Pour out Your anger Open your door and recite the prayer Sh'foch Hamatcha to show that you are free and unafraid, that you and your people are celebrating Passover for all the world to see and to witness.

Pour out Your anger Yes, Jews have long and bitter memories of the Amalekites, Romans, forced conversions, inquisitions, pogroms, lynchings, boycotts and death camps. For Jews it is a holy obligation to remember those innocent souls who lost their lives to the forces of hate. Jews must also be aware that these forces still roam the earth, sometimes directed at Jews, sometimes at Gypsies, and sometimes at people of different colors and religions. There is one people, Jews, who for the last 2,000 years have been routinely subjected to persecution, atrocities and murder by the Crusaders, Inquisition, Cossacks, Nazis, and others driven by hate.

ANI MA' AMIN

In some homes a new ceremony has been introduced before opening the door for Elijah the Prophet. During the ceremony we remember the six million Jews who were murdered by the Nazis and the heroes of the ghetto revolts.

We sing the song Ani Ma'Amin. This song of hope was sung by the martyrs in the concentration camps. The words were written in accordance with the teachings of the famous Jewish philosopher Moses Maimonides.

אֲנִי מַאֲמִין 1 I believe

אֲנִי מַאֲמִין, אֲנִי מַאֲמִין 2 I believe, I believe,

בֶּאֱמוּנָה שְׁלֵמָה, בֶּאֱמוּנָה שְׁלֵמָה 3 With all my faith,
with all my faith

בְּבִיאַת הַמָּשִׁיחַ, 4 That the Messiah will come

בְּבִיאַת הַמָּשִׁיחַ 5 That the Messiah will come

אֲנִי מַאֲמִין. 6 I believe

The Holocaust was not an overnight happening. The seeds of anti-Semitism were planted and nourished by the churches of Europe.

For centuries, the blood libel accusation, on or around Passover, resulted in the murder of hundreds of thousands of innocent Jews. Christian priests taught that Jews needed the blood of a Gentile child to make matzot. Consequently, during the Passover season, a missing, lost, or dead Christian child was an excuse for attacks against the Jewish population.

In 1144 C.E., Theobald of Cambridge, England, a converted Jew, testified that the Jews needed the blood of Christian children to make matzot. The leaders of the church eagerly accepted the outrageous lie and "proved" it when a Christian child was found dead in Norwich. The dead child was canonized as St. William.

The blood libel quickly spread through Europe, and was used as an excuse by the Crusaders to kill Jews, plunder their homes, and destroy their communities.

A few Christian leaders, such as Pope Gregory X, Pope Clement XIV, Pope Pius XI, and some Christian scholars wrote refutations, but the charge persisted.

In the 20th century, the Kishnev pogrom in Russia in 1903 followed the spread of a blood libel accusation. In this pogrom about a hundred Jews were murdered and several hundred severely wounded. Another pogrom occurred in 1905.

In 1911, a Russian Jew named Mendel Beilis was accused of committing a ritual murder. The police investigation and his trial were accompanied by violent anti-Semitic propaganda by the Russian press and government. The trial was held in Kiev in 1913, and Beilis was acquited.

Even today, in some parts of Europe, the Passover season still awakens blood libel accusations.

הַלֵּל   HALLEL (13)

Psalm 115:1-11

1 לֹא לָנוּ יְיָ, לֹא לָנוּ, כִּי־לְשִׁמְךָ תֵּן כָּבוֹד. עַל־חַסְדְּךָ עַל־

2 אֲמִתֶּךָ: לָמָּה יֹאמְרוּ הַגּוֹיִם, אַיֵּה־נָא אֱלֹהֵיהֶם: וֵאלֹהֵינוּ

3 בַשָּׁמָיִם, כֹּל אֲשֶׁר־חָפֵץ עָשָׂה: עֲצַבֵּיהֶם כֶּסֶף וְזָהָב, מַעֲשֵׂה

4 יְדֵי אָדָם: פֶּה־לָהֶם וְלֹא יְדַבֵּרוּ, עֵינַיִם לָהֶם וְלֹא יִרְאוּ:

5 אָזְנַיִם לָהֶם וְלֹא יִשְׁמָעוּ, אַף לָהֶם וְלֹא יְרִיחוּן: יְדֵיהֶם

6 וְלֹא יְמִישׁוּן, רַגְלֵיהֶם וְלֹא יְהַלֵּכוּ, לֹא־יֶהְגּוּ בִּגְרוֹנָם:

7 כְּמוֹהֶם יִהְיוּ עֹשֵׂיהֶם, כֹּל אֲשֶׁר־בֹּטֵחַ בָּהֶם: יִשְׂרָאֵל בְּטַח

8 בַּיְיָ, עֶזְרָם וּמָגִנָּם הוּא: בֵּית אַהֲרֹן בִּטְחוּ בַיְיָ, עֶזְרָם וּמָגִנָּם

9 הוּא: יִרְאֵי יְיָ בִּטְחוּ בַיְיָ, עֶזְרָם וּמָגִנָּם הוּא:

Psalm 115:12-18

10 יְיָ זְכָרָנוּ יְבָרֵךְ, יְבָרֵךְ אֶת־בֵּית יִשְׂרָאֵל. יְבָרֵךְ אֶת־בֵּית

11 אַהֲרֹן: יְבָרֵךְ יִרְאֵי יְיָ, הַקְּטַנִּים עִם־הַגְּדֹלִים: יֹסֵף יְיָ עֲלֵיכֶם,

12 עֲלֵיכֶם וְעַל־בְּנֵיכֶם: בְּרוּכִים אַתֶּם לַיְיָ, עֹשֵׂה שָׁמַיִם וָאָרֶץ:

13 הַשָּׁמַיִם שָׁמַיִם לַיְיָ, וְהָאָרֶץ נָתַן לִבְנֵי־אָדָם: לֹא־הַמֵּתִים

14 יְהַלְלוּ־יָהּ, וְלֹא כָּל־יֹרְדֵי דוּמָה: וַאֲנַחְנוּ נְבָרֵךְ יָהּ, מֵעַתָּה

15 וְעַד־עוֹלָם הַלְלוּיָהּ:

The House of Aaron Moses and Aaron were members of the tribe of Levi. All priests and Levites are descendants of the tribe of Levi. Aaron and his descendants were given the honor of the priesthood because he was the brother of Moses and helped free the Hebrews from slavery.

HALLEL (13)

Psalm 115:1-11

Not to us, O Eternal, not to us,
But to Your name give glory,
For Your mercy and truth.
Why should the nations say,
"Where, now, is their God?"
Our God is in heaven
And He does what He wills.
Their idols are of silver and gold,
The work of human hands.
They have a mouth but speak not;
They have eyes but see not;
They have ears but cannot hear;
They have a nose but cannot smell;
They have hands but cannot feel;
They have feet but cannot walk;
They make no sound in their throat;
Those who make idols become like them,
And so will those who trust in them.
O Israel, trust in the Eternal;
The Eternal is their help and their shield.
House of Aaron, trust in the Lord
He is your help and shield.

Psalm 115:12-18

The Eternal remembers us;
And will bless the House of Israel
And the House of Aaron.
The Lord will bless those who revere the Eternal,
The lowly and the great.
May the Eternal enlarge your family.
Blessed are you of the Eternal,
The maker of heaven and earth.
The heavens belong to the Eternal,
And the earth to mankind.
The dead cannot praise the Eternal,
They have gone down to silence.
But we will bless the Eternal,
Forever and forever.
Halleluyah! Praise the Eternal.

אָהַבְתִּי כִּי־יִשְׁמַע יְיָ, אֶת־קוֹלִי תַּחֲנוּנָי: כִּי־הִטָּה אָזְנוֹ לִי, 1

וּבְיָמַי אֶקְרָא: אֲפָפוּנִי חֶבְלֵי־מָוֶת, וּמְצָרֵי שְׁאוֹל מְצָאוּנִי, 2

צָרָה וְיָגוֹן אֶמְצָא: וּבְשֵׁם־יְיָ אֶקְרָא, אָנָּה יְיָ מַלְּטָה נַפְשִׁי: 3

חַנּוּן יְיָ וְצַדִּיק, וֵאלֹהֵינוּ מְרַחֵם: שֹׁמֵר פְּתָאיִם יְיָ, דַּלּוֹתִי 4

וְלִי יְהוֹשִׁיעַ: שׁוּבִי נַפְשִׁי לִמְנוּחָיְכִי, כִּי יְיָ גָּמַל עָלָיְכִי: כִּי 5

חִלַּצְתָּ נַפְשִׁי מִמָּוֶת, אֶת־עֵינִי מִן־דִּמְעָה, אֶת־רַגְלִי מִדֶּחִי: 6

אֶתְהַלֵּךְ לִפְנֵי יְיָ, בְּאַרְצוֹת הַחַיִּים: הֶאֱמַנְתִּי כִּי אֲדַבֵּר, 7

אֲנִי עָנִיתִי מְאֹד: אֲנִי אָמַרְתִּי בְחָפְזִי, כָּל־הָאָדָם כֹּזֵב: 8

Psalm 116:12-19

מָה־אָשִׁיב לַיְיָ, כָּל־תַּגְמוּלוֹהִי עָלָי: כּוֹס־יְשׁוּעוֹת אֶשָּׂא, 9

וּבְשֵׁם יְיָ אֶקְרָא: נְדָרַי לַיְיָ אֲשַׁלֵּם, נֶגְדָה־נָּא לְכָל־עַמּוֹ: 10

יָקָר בְּעֵינֵי יְיָ, הַמָּוְתָה לַחֲסִידָיו: אָנָּה יְיָ כִּי־אֲנִי עַבְדֶּךָ, אֲנִי 11

עַבְדְּךָ בֶּן־אֲמָתֶךָ, פִּתַּחְתָּ לְמוֹסֵרָי: לְךָ־אֶזְבַּח זֶבַח תּוֹדָה, 12

וּבְשֵׁם יְיָ אֶקְרָא: נְדָרַי לַיְיָ אֲשַׁלֵּם, נֶגְדָה־נָּא לְכָל־עַמּוֹ: 13

בְּחַצְרוֹת בֵּית יְיָ, בְּתוֹכֵכִי יְרוּשָׁלָיִם, הַלְלוּיָהּ: 14

Tehillim, the Book of Psalms The Book of Psalms, consisting of 150 hymns, is the first book of the third division of the Bible, known as the Ketuvim or Sacred Writings. The name Tehillim means "praises." The psalms are songs of praise arranged to be sung to the accompaniment of the Temple musicians. Tradition assigns the authorship of the psalms to King David. These liturgical poems are the finest religious poetry ever produced by any nation. They are unique because of the majesty of their language, and its inspirational and spiritual expression. Today, some religious Jews recite a different psalm every day.

In the presence of all the people It is an obligation of all Jewish people to identify with and participate in Jewish religious and communal affairs. In numbers there is strength. When Jews speak with one voice, the community, the state, the country, and the world listen.

I love the Eternal
> because the Eternal has heard my voice.
>> And my pleas,
> Because God listens to me.
>> I will call upon the Lord all my days.
> <u>The snare of death.</u>
>> Torment of the grave seized me,
> Trouble and sorrow met me.
>> But I called upon the name of the Eternal,
> "Eternal I beg You, save me."
>> Gracious is the Eternal and righteous to us;
> The Eternal is merciful.
>> The Eternal watches over the simple:
> I was brought low and He saved me.
>> Be at rest again. O my soul,
> For the Eternal has dealt bountifully with you.
>> For You, O Eternal, have saved me from death.
> My eye from tears
>> And my foot from stumbling.
> I had faith even when I said,
>> "I am greatly afflicted."
> Only in haste did I say.
>> "all men are untrustworthy"
>> *Psalm 116:12-19*

How can I repay the Eternal
> For all His goodness to me?
>> I will lift up the cup of salvation,
> And proclaim the name of the Eternal.
>> My vows to the Eternal I will fulfill;
> Would it were <u>in the presence of all the people!</u>
>> Costly in the eyes of the Eternal
> is the death of His pious servants.
>> I pray, O Eternal, for I am Your servant.
> I am Your servant, child of Your handmaid:
>> You have loosed my bonds.
> To You I will offer thanksgiving.
>> And call on the name of the Eternal.
> My vows to the Eternal I will fulfill.
>> Would it were in the presence of all His people.

Psalm 117

הַלְלוּ אֶת־יְיָ כָּל־גּוֹיִם, שַׁבְּחוּהוּ כָּל־הָאֻמִּים: כִּי גָבַר עָלֵינוּ 1

חַסְדּוֹ, וֶאֱמֶת־יְיָ לְעוֹלָם, הַלְלוּיָהּ: 2

Psalm 118

הוֹדוּ לַיְיָ כִּי־טוֹב.   כִּי לְעוֹלָם חַסְדּוֹ: 3

יֹאמַר־נָא יִשְׂרָאֵל.   כִּי לְעוֹלָם חַסְדּוֹ: 4

יֹאמְרוּ־נָא בֵית־אַהֲרֹן.   כִּי לְעוֹלָם חַסְדּוֹ: 5

יֹאמְרוּ־נָא יִרְאֵי יְיָ.   כִּי לְעוֹלָם חַסְדּוֹ: 6

מִן־הַמֵּצַר קָרָאתִי יָּהּ, עָנָנִי בַמֶּרְחַב יָהּ: יְיָ לִי לֹא אִירָא, 7

מַה־יַּעֲשֶׂה לִי אָדָם: יְיָ לִי בְּעֹזְרָי, וַאֲנִי אֶרְאֶה בְשֹׂנְאָי: 8

טוֹב לַחֲסוֹת בַּיְיָ, מִבְּטֹחַ בָּאָדָם: טוֹב לַחֲסוֹת בַּיְיָ, מִבְּטֹחַ 9

בִּנְדִיבִים: כָּל־גּוֹיִם סְבָבוּנִי, בְּשֵׁם יְיָ כִּי אֲמִילַם: סַבּוּנִי 10

גַם־סְבָבוּנִי, בְּשֵׁם יְיָ כִּי אֲמִילַם: סַבּוּנִי כִדְבֹרִים, דֹּעֲכוּ 11

כְּאֵשׁ קוֹצִים, בְּשֵׁם יְיָ כִּי אֲמִילַם: דָּחֹה דְחִיתַנִי לִנְפֹּל, וַיְיָ 12

עֲזָרָנִי: עָזִּי וְזִמְרָת יָהּ, וַיְהִי־לִי לִישׁוּעָה: קוֹל רִנָּה וִישׁוּעָה, 13

בְּאָהֳלֵי צַדִּיקִים, יְמִין יְיָ עֹשָׂה חָיִל: יְמִין יְיָ רוֹמֵמָה, יְמִין 14

יְיָ עֹשָׂה חָיִל: 15

Psalm 117 This is the shortest of the 150 psalms. It has only 16 words. The psalm states the hope that all nations will ultimately be united in the pure worship of Adonai.

Psalm 118 This is the last and most joyful of the Hallel psalms.

Psalm 117

Praise the Eternal, all nations,
Praise God, all peoples,
For God's mercy is great,
God's truth is forever.
Halleluyah: Praise the Eternal.

Psalm 118

Give thanks to the Eternal for God is good,
God's mercy is forever.
Let Israel say: God's mercy is forever.
Let the House of <u>Aaron</u> say:
God's mercy lasts forever.
Let those who honor the Eternal say:
God's mercy is forever.

Out of my distress I called upon the Eternal:
The Eternal answered by setting me free.
The Eternal is with me, I do not fear.
What can people do to me? When the Eternal is my helper,
I shall be victorious over my enemies.
In the courts of the Eternal,
It is better to trust in the Eternal than to rely on people.
It is better to trust in the Eternal
Than to rely on princes.
Nations surround me:
In the name of the Eternal I will cut them down.
They surround me like bees;
They will be extinguished as a fire of thorns;
In the name of the Eternal I will surely cut them down.
They thrust at me so as to make me fall.
But the Eternal supports me.
The Eternal is my strength and my song,
The Eternal has become my salvation.
The joyous song of victory is heard. In the tents of the righteous,
The right hand of the Eternal is sturdy.
I shall not die, but live.

Aaron Moses consecrated Aaron and his sons for the priesthood by anointing their heads with oil. Forever after, Aaron, his sons, and their descendants would be the priests (Kohanim) of Israel. The duties of the priests were many and varied. Most important, they offered sacrifices for the people and raised their voices in prayer. The priestly robes were prescribed in the Torah. For Aaron, the high priest, it included a breastplate bearing the Urim and Tumim, twelve precious stones in four rows, each stone symbolizing one of the tribes of Israel. The high priest wore these garments when he served in the Temple.

1 לֹא־אָמוּת כִּי־אֶחְיֶה, וַאֲסַפֵּר מַעֲשֵׂי יָהּ: יַסֹּר יִסְּרַנִּי יָּהּ,

2 וְלַמָּוֶת לֹא נְתָנָנִי: פִּתְחוּ־לִי שַׁעֲרֵי־צֶדֶק, אָבֹא־בָם אוֹדֶה

3 יָּהּ: זֶה־הַשַּׁעַר לַיְיָ, צַדִּיקִים יָבֹאוּ בוֹ:

4 אוֹדְךָ כִּי עֲנִיתָנִי, וַתְּהִי־לִי לִישׁוּעָה: אוֹדְךָ כִּי עֲנִיתָנִי,

5 וַתְּהִי־לִי לִישׁוּעָה: אֶבֶן מָאֲסוּ הַבּוֹנִים, הָיְתָה לְרֹאשׁ פִּנָּה:

6 אֶבֶן מָאֲסוּ הַבּוֹנִים, הָיְתָה לְרֹאשׁ פִּנָּה: מֵאֵת יְיָ הָיְתָה

7 זֹּאת, הִיא נִפְלָאת בְּעֵינֵינוּ: מֵאֵת יְיָ הָיְתָה זֹּאת, הִיא

8 נִפְלָאת בְּעֵינֵינוּ: זֶה־הַיּוֹם עָשָׂה יְיָ, נָגִילָה וְנִשְׂמְחָה בוֹ:

9 זֶה־הַיּוֹם עָשָׂה יְיָ, נָגִילָה וְנִשְׂמְחָה בוֹ:

10 אָנָּא יְיָ הוֹשִׁיעָה נָּא:

11 אָנָּא יְיָ הוֹשִׁיעָה נָּא:

12 אָנָּא יְיָ הַצְלִיחָה נָּא:

13 אָנָּא יְיָ הַצְלִיחָה נָּא:

14 בָּרוּךְ הַבָּא בְּשֵׁם יְיָ, בֵּרַכְנוּכֶם מִבֵּית יְיָ: בָּרוּךְ הַבָּא בְּשֵׁם יְיָ,

15 בֵּרַכְנוּכֶם מִבֵּית יְיָ: אֵל יְיָ וַיָּאֶר לָנוּ, אִסְרוּ־חַג בַּעֲבֹתִים,

16 עַד־קַרְנוֹת הַמִּזְבֵּחַ: אֵל יְיָ וַיָּאֶר לָנוּ, אִסְרוּ־חַג בַּעֲבֹתִים,

17 עַד־קַרְנוֹת הַמִּזְבֵּחַ: אֵלִי אַתָּה וְאוֹדֶךָּ, אֱלֹהַי אֲרוֹמְמֶךָּ:

18 אֵלִי אַתָּה וְאוֹדֶךָּ, אֱלֹהַי אֲרוֹמְמֶךָּ: הוֹדוּ לַיְיָ כִּי־טוֹב, כִּי

19 לְעוֹלָם חַסְדּוֹ: הוֹדוּ לַיְיָ כִּי־טוֹב, כִּי לְעוֹלָם חַסְדּוֹ:

The stone Israel, rejected, denigrated, and abused by the nations of the world, is destined to be the foundation stone in the Kingdom of God.

The stone According to the Midrash, the construction of the world began with the foundation stone (*even shetiyah*) of the Temple in Jerusalem. The Temple was located in the center of Jerusalem, Jerusalem is located in the center of Israel, and the Holy Land is in the center of the earth.

And acknowledge the works of the Eternal.
Though the Eternal has punished me,
The Lord has not given me over to death.
Open the gates of righteousness,
I will enter them to praise the Eternal.
This is the gate of the Eternal,
The righteous shall enter through it

I will give thanks to You, for You have answered me,
And become my salvation.
<u>The stone</u> which the builders rejected
Has become the cornerstone.
This is the work of the Lord,
It is marvelous in our eyes.
This is the day Lord has made;
Let us rejoice and be glad in it.

O Lord, we beseech You, save us,
O Lord, we beseech You, save us.
O Lord, we beseech You, prosper us.
O Lord, we beseech You, prosper us.

Blessed be the person who comes in the name of the Eternal;
We bless you from the house of the Eternal.
The Eternal has given us light;
Bring the sacrifice wrapped with myrtle leaves to the altar.
You are my God and I will praise You:
Give thanks to the Eternal, for He is good;
For His mercy endures forever.

The stone The full Hebrew name is *even shetiyah* (the foundation stone).
This is the projecting rock on the summit on the Temple Mount in
Jerusalem. Legend says that this stone is the focal point of the world,
from which the world was created. Jewish tradition believes that Isaac was
bound for sacrifice on this rock. According to the Mishnah, in the First
and Second Temples, the Holy Ark and the Tablets of the Ten
Commandments were placed upon it. The Mishnah dates the placing of
the stone to the time of the construction of the First Temple. Other
sources ignore the view that creation was initiated at the *even shetiyah*.
Today the *even shetiyah*, which is revered by Islam, can be seen in the
Mosque of Omar.

כִּי לְעוֹלָם חַסְדּוֹ:	1 הוֹדוּ לַייָ כִּי־טוֹב,
כִּי לְעוֹלָם חַסְדּוֹ:	2 הוֹדוּ לֵאלֹהֵי הָאֱלֹהִים,
כִּי לְעוֹלָם חַסְדּוֹ:	3 הוֹדוּ לַאֲדֹנֵי הָאֲדֹנִים,
כִּי לְעוֹלָם חַסְדּוֹ:	4 לְעֹשֵׂה נִפְלָאוֹת גְּדֹלוֹת לְבַדּוֹ,
כִּי לְעוֹלָם חַסְדּוֹ:	5 לְעֹשֵׂה הַשָּׁמַיִם בִּתְבוּנָה,
כִּי לְעוֹלָם חַסְדּוֹ:	6 לְרֹקַע הָאָרֶץ עַל־הַמָּיִם,
כִּי לְעוֹלָם חַסְדּוֹ:	7 לְעֹשֵׂה אוֹרִים גְּדֹלִים,
כִּי לְעוֹלָם חַסְדּוֹ:	8 אֶת־הַשֶּׁמֶשׁ לְמֶמְשֶׁלֶת בַּיּוֹם,
9 אֶת־הַיָּרֵחַ וְכוֹכָבִים לְמֶמְשְׁלוֹת בַּלָּיְלָה, כִּי לְעוֹלָם חַסְדּוֹ:	
כִּי לְעוֹלָם חַסְדּוֹ:	10 לְמַכֵּה מִצְרַיִם בִּבְכוֹרֵיהֶם,
כִּי לְעוֹלָם חַסְדּוֹ:	11 וַיּוֹצֵא יִשְׂרָאֵל מִתּוֹכָם,
כִּי לְעוֹלָם חַסְדּוֹ:	12 בְּיָד חֲזָקָה וּבִזְרוֹעַ נְטוּיָה,
כִּי לְעוֹלָם חַסְדּוֹ:	13 לְגֹזֵר יַם־סוּף לִגְזָרִים,
כִּי לְעוֹלָם חַסְדּוֹ:	14 וְהֶעֱבִיר יִשְׂרָאֵל בְּתוֹכוֹ,

The wilderness The Children of Israel wandered through the wilderness of Sinai for 40 years. It was here, in the barren, burning wasteland, that the diverse group of slaves were hammered and forged into a strong and cohesive nation, Israel.

The Sinai Desert is a peninsula which lies between the Gulf of Aqaba on the east and Suez on the left. It has a triangular shape and is 150 miles wide and 250 miles long. The area for a time was claimed by several Egyptian dynasties and was valued for its turquoise and copper mines. During the Yom Kippur War in 1973, the Israelis captured the Sinai peninsula from the Egyptians. As part of the peace treaty of 1979, the Israelis returned the Sinai to the Egyptians.

PSALM 136

Give thanks to the Eternal, for the Eternal is good;

For the Eternal's mercy endures forever.

Give thanks to the Eternal of Gods;

For the Eternal's mercy endures forever.

Give thanks to the Eternal of lords;

For the Eternal's mercy endures forever.

To the Eternal who alone performs great miracles;

For the Eternal's mercy endures forever.

To Him Who made the heavens with wisdom;

For the Eternal's mercy endures forever.

To the Eternal who placed the earth above the waters;

For the Eternal's mercy endures forever.

To the Eternal who made the great lights;

For the Eternal's mercy endures forever.

The sun to rule by day;

For the Eternal's mercy endures forever.

The moon and stars to rule by night;

For the Eternal's mercy endures forever.

To the Eternal Who punished Egypt through their firstborn;

For the Eternal's mercy endures forever.

And brought Israel forth from among them;

For the Eternal's mercy endures forever.

To the Eternal Who parted the Red Sea;

For the Eternal's mercy endures forever.

Who drowned Pharaoh and his army in the Red Sea;

For the Eternal's mercy endures forever.

To the Eternal who led the Hebrews through the wilderness;

For the Eternal's mercy endures forever.

Gives thanks to the Eternal This psalm is called the Great Hallel since it includes praises to God for creating the world and for the miracle on behalf of Israel. Because the psalm mentions the miracle of the Exodus and splitting of the Red Sea, it was included in the Haggadah.

כִּי לְעוֹלָם חַסְדּוֹ:	1 וְנִעֵר פַּרְעֹה וְחֵילוֹ בְיַם־סוּף,
כִּי לְעוֹלָם חַסְדּוֹ:	2 לְמוֹלִיךְ עַמּוֹ בַּמִּדְבָּר,
כִּי לְעוֹלָם חַסְדּוֹ:	3 לְמַכֵּה מְלָכִים גְּדֹלִים,
כִּי לְעוֹלָם חַסְדּוֹ:	4 וַיַּהֲרֹג מְלָכִים אַדִּירִים,
כִּי לְעוֹלָם חַסְדּוֹ:	5 לְסִיחוֹן מֶלֶךְ הָאֱמֹרִי,
כִּי לְעוֹלָם חַסְדּוֹ:	6 וּלְעוֹג מֶלֶךְ הַבָּשָׁן,
כִּי לְעוֹלָם חַסְדּוֹ:	7 וְנָתַן אַרְצָם לְנַחֲלָה,
כִּי לְעוֹלָם חַסְדּוֹ:	8 נַחֲלָה לְיִשְׂרָאֵל עַבְדּוֹ,
כִּי לְעוֹלָם חַסְדּוֹ:	9 שֶׁבְּשִׁפְלֵנוּ זָכַר־לָנוּ,
כִּי לְעוֹלָם חַסְדּוֹ:	10 וַיִּפְרְקֵנוּ מִצָּרֵינוּ,
כִּי לְעוֹלָם חַסְדּוֹ:	11 נֹתֵן לֶחֶם לְכָל־בָּשָׂר,
כִּי לְעוֹלָם חַסְדּוֹ:	12 הוֹדוּ לְאֵל הַשָּׁמָיִם,

Sihon, king of the Amorites The Children of Israel wandered in the desert for 40 years. When they wanted to pass through settled lands, Moses would send a message to the king and ask permisson.
When they came to the land of the Amorites, Moses sent the usual message to King Sihon. His reply was a flat refusal. Sihon assembled his army to drive off the peaceful Israelites.
But this new generation of Hebrews were hardened by the desert and better trained than their slave parents. They stood their ground and routed the Amorites.

To the Eternal Who punished great kings;
For the Eternal's mercy endures forever.
And slew mighty kings;
For the Eternal's mercy endures forever.
<u>Sihon, king of the Amorites;</u>
For the Eternal's mercy endures forever.
And <u>Og, king of Bashan;</u>
For the Eternal's mercy endures forever.
And gave their land as an inheritance;
For the Eternal's mercy endures forever.
Who remembered us in our humilty;
For the Eternal's mercy endures forever.
And saved us from those who trampled us;
For the Eternal's mercy lasts forever.
Who gives food to all;
For the Eternal's mercy endures forever.
Gives thanks to the God of the heavens;
For the Eternal's mercy lasts forever.

Og, king of Bashan Og was an Amorite king who tried to stop the march of the Israelites through the desert but was defeated. From there they continued their march and traveled to the plains of Moab and camped on the east side of the Jordan River, opposite the city of Jericho. It was from this area that Joshua eventually launched the invasion of the Promised Land. Some of the Israelites settled and made their home on the east side of the Jordan River.

NISHMAT KOL CHAI

1 נִשְׁמַת כָּל־חַי תְּבָרֵךְ אֶת־שִׁמְךָ יְיָ אֱלֹהֵינוּ. וְרוּחַ כָּל־בָּשָׂר תְּפָאֵר וּתְרוֹמֵם

2 זִכְרְךָ מַלְכֵּנוּ תָּמִיד. מִן־הָעוֹלָם וְעַד־הָעוֹלָם אַתָּה אֵל, וּמִבַּלְעָדֶיךָ אֵין

3 לָנוּ מֶלֶךְ גּוֹאֵל וּמוֹשִׁיעַ פּוֹדֶה וּמַצִּיל וּמְפַרְנֵס וּמְרַחֵם בְּכָל־עֵת צָרָה

4 וְצוּקָה. אֵין לָנוּ מֶלֶךְ אֶלָּא אָתָּה:

5 אֱלֹהֵי הָרִאשׁוֹנִים וְהָאַחֲרוֹנִים אֱלֽוֹהַּ כָּל־בְּרִיּוֹת, אֲדוֹן כָּל־תּוֹלָדוֹת

6 הַמְהֻלָּל בְּרֹב הַתִּשְׁבָּחוֹת הַמְנַהֵג עוֹלָמוֹ בְּחֶסֶד וּבְרִיּוֹתָיו בְּרַחֲמִים.

7 וַיְיָ עֵר הִנֵּה לֹא־יָנוּם וְלֹא יִישָׁן. הַמְעוֹרֵר יְשֵׁנִים וְהַמֵּקִיץ נִרְדָּמִים

8 וְהַמֵּשִׂיחַ אִלְּמִים וְהַמַּתִּיר אֲסוּרִים וְהַסּוֹמֵךְ נוֹפְלִים וְהַזּוֹקֵף כְּפוּפִים

9 וּלְךָ לְבַדְּךָ אֲנַחְנוּ מוֹדִים: וְאִלּוּ פִינוּ מָלֵא שִׁירָה כַּיָּם,

10 וּלְשׁוֹנֵנוּ רִנָּה כַּהֲמוֹן גַּלָּיו וְשִׂפְתוֹתֵינוּ שֶׁבַח כְּמֶרְחֲבֵי רָקִיעַ וְעֵינֵינוּ

11 מְאִירוֹת כַּשֶּׁמֶשׁ וְכַיָּרֵחַ וְיָדֵינוּ פְרוּשׂוֹת כְּנִשְׁרֵי שָׁמָיִם וְרַגְלֵינוּ קַלּוֹת

12 כָּאַיָּלוֹת אֵין אֲנַחְנוּ מַסְפִּיקִים לְהוֹדוֹת לְךָ יְיָ אֱלֹהֵינוּ וֵאלֹהֵי אֲבוֹתֵינוּ

13 וּלְבָרֵךְ אֶת־שְׁמֶךָ עַל־אַחַת מֵאֶלֶף אֶלֶף אַלְפֵי אֲלָפִים וְרִבֵּי רְבָבוֹת

14 פְּעָמִים הַטּוֹבוֹת שֶׁעָשִׂיתָ עִם־אֲבוֹתֵינוּ וְעִמָּנוּ:

15 מִמִּצְרַיִם גְּאַלְתָּנוּ יְיָ אֱלֹהֵינוּ וּמִבֵּית עֲבָדִים פְּדִיתָנוּ. בְּרָעָב זַנְתָּנוּ וּבְשָׂבָע

16 כִּלְכַּלְתָּנוּ מֵחֶרֶב הִצַּלְתָּנוּ וּמִדֶּבֶר מִלַּטְתָּנוּ וּמֵחֳלָיִם רָעִים וְנֶאֱמָנִים

17 דִּלִּיתָנוּ: עַד־הֵנָּה עֲזָרוּנוּ רַחֲמֶיךָ, וְלֹא־עֲזָבוּנוּ חֲסָדֶיךָ. וְאַל־תִּטְּשֵׁנוּ יְיָ

18 אֱלֹהֵינוּ לָנֶצַח:

1 עַל־כֵּן אֵבָרִים שֶׁפִּלַּגְתָּ בָּנוּ וְרוּחַ וּנְשָׁמָה שֶׁנָּפַחְתָּ בְּאַפֵּינוּ וְלָשׁוֹן

2 אֲשֶׁר שַׂמְתָּ בְּפִינוּ הֵן הֵם יוֹדוּ וִיבָרְכוּ וִישַׁבְּחוּ וִיפָאֲרוּ וִירוֹמְמוּ

3 וְיַעֲרִיצוּ וְיַקְדִּישׁוּ וְיַמְלִיכוּ אֶת־שִׁמְךָ מַלְכֵּנוּ תָּמִיד: כִּי כָל־פֶּה

4 לְךָ יוֹדֶה וְכָל־לָשׁוֹן לְךָ תִשָּׁבַע וְכָל־עַיִן לְךָ תְצַפֶּה וְכָל־בֶּרֶךְ לְךָ

5 תִכְרַע וְכָל־קוֹמָה לְפָנֶיךָ תִשְׁתַּחֲוֶה. וְכָל־לְבָבוֹת יִירָאוּךָ וְכָל־קֶרֶב

6 וּכְלָיוֹת יְזַמְּרוּ לִשְׁמֶךָ כַּדָּבָר שֶׁכָּתוּב כָּל־עַצְמוֹתַי תֹּאמַרְנָה יְיָ מִי

7 כָמוֹךָ: מַצִּיל עָנִי מֵחָזָק מִמֶּנּוּ וְעָנִי וְאֶבְיוֹן מִגּוֹזְלוֹ:

Nishmat The Nishmat prayer is a beautiful poem praising the power of the Eternal. The prayer is mentiond in the Talmud, but its authorship is unknown. Today, Nishmat is recited on Sabbaths and festivals.

THE SOUL OF EVERY LIVING THING

The soul of every living thing blesses Your name. Eternal God,
the spirit of all flesh adores and glorifies Your name, our Ruler.
Forever and ever You are God, and besides You we have no ruler
Who redeems and helps us. Who is merciful in every time of
sorrow and distress; we have no Ruler except You.

O God of the beginning and of the end, God of all creatures,
Master of all existence, Who is praised with many praises,
Who leads the world with loving-kindness, and the creatures
with mercy: God Who slumbers nor sleeps not, awakens the
sleeping and stirs the slumbering, gives speech to the silent
and releases the imprisoned, supports the fallen and upholds
the weak, to You alone we give thanks.

Were our mouths filled with singing as the sea, and our
voice uplifted in song as the waves, and our lips with praise as
the heavens, and our eyes shining as the sun and the moon,
and our hands stretched out as the eagles of the skies, and our
feet swift as the deer, we would still not be able to offer proper
thanks to You, Eternal our God, and God of our ancestors and
to praise Your Name and for the happy times You gave our
forefathers and us.

From Egypt You redeemed us, and from the house of bondage
you freed us. In famine You fed us, in plenty You supported us,
from the sword You saved us, from pestilence You protected
us, from severe sickness You spared us. Do not forsake us, we
pray, Eternal our God.

The limbs You have fashioned within us, and the spirit of
life which You have breathed into us, and the tongue which You
have placed in our mouth, they shall all thank, praise, extol,
glorify, exalt, adore, hallow, and give sovereignty to Your Name,
for every mouth shall give thanks to You, and every tongue shall
pledge loyalty to You; and every knee shall bend to You, and every
living being shall bow down to You; all hearts shall revere You, and
all beings shall sing to Your Name, as it is written: "All my being
shall say, Eternal, who is like You, delivering the weak from the
strong, and the needy from the oppressor."

The soul of every living thing There is no solid evidence of the
authorship for this prayer. However, there is a disputed legend that it was
composed by a Gentile priest who returned to Judaism when he
discovered that he had been born a Jew. He composed this poem in which
he writes: "We have no ruler except You," meaning the God of Israel.

1 מִי יִדְמֶה־לָּךְ וּמִי יִשְׁוֶה־לָּךְ וּמִי יַעֲרָךְ־לָךְ. הָאֵל הַגָּדוֹל הַגִּבּוֹר

2 וְהַנּוֹרָא אֵל עֶלְיוֹן, קֹנֵה שָׁמַיִם וָאָרֶץ: נְהַלֶּלְךָ וּנְשַׁבֵּחֲךָ וּנְפָאֶרְךָ

3 וּנְבָרֵךְ אֶת־שֵׁם קָדְשֶׁךָ כָּאָמוּר. לְדָוִד בָּרְכִי נַפְשִׁי אֶת־יְיָ וְכָל־קְרָבַי

4 אֶת־שֵׁם קָדְשׁוֹ:

5 הָאֵל בְּתַעֲצֻמוֹת עֻזֶּךָ הַגָּדוֹל בִּכְבוֹד שְׁמֶךָ הַגִּבּוֹר לָנֶצַח וְהַנּוֹרָא

6 בְּנוֹרְאוֹתֶיךָ: הַמֶּלֶךְ הַיּוֹשֵׁב עַל־כִּסֵּא רָם וְנִשָּׂא:

7 שׁוֹכֵן־עַד מָרוֹם וְקָדוֹשׁ שְׁמוֹ. וְכָתוּב. רַנְּנוּ צַדִּיקִים בַּיָי לַיְשָׁרִים

8 נָאוָה תְהִלָּה:

9 בְּפִי יְשָׁרִים תִּתְרוֹמָם וּבְשִׂפְתֵי צַדִּיקִים תִּתְבָּרַךְ וּבִלְשׁוֹן חֲסִידִים

10 תִּתְקַדָּשׁ וּבְקֶרֶב קְדוֹשִׁים תִּתְהַלָּל:

11 וּבְמַקְהֲלוֹת רִבְבוֹת עַמְּךָ בֵּית יִשְׂרָאֵל בְּרִנָּה יִתְפָּאַר שִׁמְךָ מַלְכֵּנוּ

12 בְּכָל־דּוֹר וָדוֹר. שֶׁכֵּן חוֹבַת כָּל־הַיְצוּרִים. לְפָנֶיךָ יְיָ אֱלֹהֵינוּ וֵאלֹהֵי

13 אֲבוֹתֵינוּ לְהוֹדוֹת לְהַלֵּל לְשַׁבֵּחַ לְפָאֵר לְרוֹמֵם לְהַדֵּר לְבָרֵךְ

14 לְעַלֵּה וּלְקַלֵּס עַל־כָּל־דִּבְרֵי שִׁירוֹת וְתִשְׁבְּחוֹת דָּוִד בֶּן־יִשַׁי עַבְדְּךָ

15 מְשִׁיחֶךָ:

16 יִשְׁתַּבַּח שִׁמְךָ לָעַד, מַלְכֵּנוּ. הָאֵל הַמֶּלֶךְ הַגָּדוֹל וְהַקָּדוֹשׁ בַּשָּׁמַיִם

17 וּבָאָרֶץ. כִּי־לְךָ נָאֶה יְיָ אֱלֹהֵינוּ וֵאלֹהֵי אֲבוֹתֵינוּ שִׁיר וּשְׁבָחָה,

18 הַלֵּל וְזִמְרָה, עֹז וּמֶמְשָׁלָה, נֶצַח גְּדֻלָּה וּגְבוּרָה, תְּהִלָּה וְתִפְאֶרֶת,

19 קְדֻשָּׁה וּמַלְכוּת, בְּרָכוֹת וְהוֹדָאוֹת מֵעַתָּה וְעַד־עוֹלָם:

20 יְהַלְלוּךָ יְיָ אֱלֹהֵינוּ (עַל) כָּל־מַעֲשֶׂיךָ, וַחֲסִידֶיךָ צַדִּיקִים עוֹשֵׂי

21 רְצוֹנֶךָ, וְכָל עַמְּךָ בֵּית יִשְׂרָאֵל בְּרִנָּה יוֹדוּ, וִיבָרְכוּ, וִישַׁבְּחוּ וִיפָאֲרוּ,

22 וִירוֹמְמוּ, וְיַעֲרִיצוּ, וְיַקְדִּישׁוּ, וְיַמְלִיכוּ אֶת שִׁמְךָ מַלְכֵּנוּ, כִּי לְךָ טוֹב

24 לְהוֹדוֹת, וּלְשִׁמְךָ נָאֶה לְזַמֵּר, כִּי מֵעוֹלָם וְעַד עוֹלָם אַתָּה אֵל:

25 בָּרוּךְ אַתָּה יְיָ, מֶלֶךְ מְהֻלָּל בַּתִּשְׁבָּחוֹת:

Who is like You, and who can equal You? Who can compare with You, O God, great, mighty, revered supreme God, Master of heaven and earth? Let us praise and worship, glorify, and bless your holy Name, as it is said by David: "O my soul, bless the Eternal, and all that is within me, bless the holy Name."

You are the Eternal by the power of Your might, great by the glory of Your name, almighty forever and inspiring awe by Your deeds. You are the Ruler who sits sublimely and exalted.

You Who dwell in eternity, exalted and holy is Your Name. And it is written: "Rejoice in the Eternal, for it becomes the upright to speak and praise."

By the mouth of the upright You shall be lauded, and by the words of the righteous You shall be praised; by the tongue of the pious You shall be exalted, and in the midst of the holy You shall be hallowed.

In the assemblies of the multitudes of Your people, the House of Israel, Your Name, O our Ruler, shall be glorified with song in every generation. For it is the duty of all creatures to give thanks, to praise, to bless, and to adore You, O Eternal our God, and the God of our ancestors, in the words of the psalms of David the son of Jesse, Your anointed servant.

May Your Name be praised forever, Who is great and holy in the heavens and on the earth: for to you, Eternal our God and God of our ancestors, it is proper to recite song and praise, prayer and psalm, strength and rule, victory, glory and might, praise and beauty, holiness and sovereignty, blessings and thanksgivings, from now and forever.

Eternal Ruler, praised be Your Name forever, You who rule in the heaven and earth. For to You, O Eternal, God of our ancestors, it is fitting to praise in song, hymn, and psalm, expressing power, eternity, greatness, holiness, blessings and thankgiving, from now and forever. O Eternal, blessed are You.

O'Eternal, may all creation praise You: May the holy ones, the righteous ones who do Your will, all Your people of the House of Israel, shall thank, bless, praise, glorify, revere and sanctify Your name with joyful song. It is good to give thanks and to sing to Your glory. Forever and ever, You are our God. Praised are You, O' Eternal our God.

On the first Seder night

וּבְכֵן וַיְהִי בַּחֲצִי הַלַּיְלָה:

1 אָז רוֹב־נִסִּים הִפְלֵאתָ בַּלַּיְלָה. בְּרֹאשׁ אַשְׁמֹרֶת זֶה הַלַּיְלָה. גֵּר־צֶדֶק

2 נִצַּחְתּוֹ כְּנֶחֱלַק לוֹ לַיְלָה.

3 וַיְהִי בַּחֲצִי הַלַּיְלָה:

4 דַּנְתָּ מֶלֶךְ גְּרָר בַּחֲלוֹם הַלַּיְלָה. הִפְחַדְתָּ אֲרַמִּי בְּאֶמֶשׁ לַיְלָה. וַיָּשַׂר

5 יִשְׂרָאֵל לְמַלְאָךְ וַיּוּכַל־לוֹ לַיְלָה.

6 וַיְהִי בַּחֲצִי הַלַּיְלָה:

7 זֶרַע בְּכוֹרֵי פַתְרוֹס מָחַצְתָּ בַּחֲצִי הַלַּיְלָה. חֵילָם לֹא־מָצְאוּ בְּקוּמָם

8 בַּלַּיְלָה. טִיסַת נְגִיד חֲרֹשֶׁת סִלִּיתָ בְּכוֹכְבֵי לַיְלָה.

9 וַיְהִי בַּחֲצִי הַלַּיְלָה:

It happened at midnight This song lists the various historical events which took place on Passover night. Each stanza ends with the refrain "It happened at midnight." Note the alphabetical arrangement of the verses.

It happened at midnight This phrase is found in the Torah in Exodus 12:29. Adonai tells Moses to prepare the Israelites for the Exodus from Egypt. And the Children of Israel did all that Moses commanded. Then "It came to pass at midnight," and in all the homes of Egypt the firstborn died, from the firstborn of Pharaoh to the firstborn of the Egyptians and the firstborn of the Egyptian cattle. Since the Egyptians worshipped animals, Adonai wished to impress them as to how powerless their gods were. In shock, the terrified Pharaoh called Moses and Aaron at night and begged them, "Rise up and take the Children of Israel and leave Egypt." And the Israelites, 600,000 in all, took their dough before it was leavened and began their momentous journey to freedom. This was the birthday of the people of Israel.

It happened at midnight The kabbalists, during the period of Isaac Luria, in the 16th century, formalized the practice of Tikkun Hazot, Midnight Prayers. The mystics recited midnight prayers in memory of the destruction of the Temple and for the restoration (*tikkun)* of the land of Israel.

The hour of midnight was chosen because David arose at midnight to study and pray. The service consists of reciting psalms.

On the first Seder night

IT HAPPENED AT MIDNIGHT !
At night, in days of old You performed many miracles
  On the first watch of this very night.
  Full victory came to Abraham,
When he divided his company at night.

IT HAPPENED AT MIDNIGHT!
At night, You judged the king of Gerar in a dream.
  You frightened Laban in the midst of the night.
At night, Israel wrestled with an angel and triumphed.

IT HAPPENED AT MIDNIGHT!
At night, You struck down the firstborn of Egypt.
  At night, they found their possessions gone when they arose.
The armies of Sisera You swept away by the stars of the night.

The armies of Sisera The Israelites in the Promised Land were frequently attacked by the Canaanites. King Jabin's army was commanded by General Sisera. Deborah, the female judge, decided that Jabin must be defeated. So she summoned a veteran warrior named Barak. He assembled an army at the top of Mount Tabor overlooking the Plain of Jezreel near the Kishon River. Jabin and Sisera assembled their chariots and their heavily armed soldiers at the foot of Mount Tabor, and waited for the Israelites to attack.
In the midst of the battle, the skies darkened and a heavy rain poured down, causing the Kishon to overflow. A raging torrent of water rushed across the plain, trapping the heavy Canaanite chariots. The Canaanite soldiers, who were weighed down with armor, were easily defeated by the lightly armed Israelites. Sisera fled, and found refuge in the tent of Jael, a Kenite. She and her husband, Hebev, were secret allies of the Israelites. While Sisera slept, Jael killed him by hammering a wooden tent peg into his temple.

138

1 יָעֵץ מְחָרֵף לְנוֹפֵף אִוּוּי הוֹבַשְׁתָּ פְּגָרָיו בַּלַּיְלָה. כָּרַע בֵּל וּמַצְּבוֹ

2 בָּאִישׁוֹן לַיְלָה. לְאִישׁ חֲמוּדוֹת נִגְלָה רָז חֶזְוֹת־לַיְלָה.

3 וַיְהִי בַּחֲצִי הַלַּיְלָה:

4 מִשְׁתַּכֵּר בִּכְלֵי קֹדֶשׁ נֶהֱרַג בּוֹ בַּלַּיְלָה. נוֹשַׁע מִבּוֹר אֲרָיוֹת פּוֹתֵר

5 בְּעֻתוּתֵי לַיְלָה. שִׂנְאָה נָטַר אֲגָגִי וְכָתַב סְפָרִים בַּלַּיְלָה.

6 וַיְהִי בַּחֲצִי הַלַּיְלָה:

7 עוֹרַרְתָּ נִצְחֲךָ עָלָיו בְּנֶדֶד שְׁנַת לַיְלָה. פּוּרָה תִדְרוֹךְ לְשׁוֹמֵר

8 מַה־מִּלַּיְלָה. צָרַח כַּשּׁוֹמֵר וְשָׂח אָתָא בֹקֶר וְגַם לָיְלָה.

9 וַיְהִי בַּחֲצִי הַלַּיְלָה:

10 קָרֵב יוֹם, אֲשֶׁר הוּא לֹא־יוֹם וְלֹא לַיְלָה. רָם הוֹדַע כִּי־לְךָ הַיּוֹם אַף

11 לְךָ הַלַּיְלָה. שׁוֹמְרִים הַפְקֵד לְעִירְךָ כָּל־הַיּוֹם וְכָל־הַלַּיְלָה. תָּאִיר

12 כְּאוֹר יוֹם חֶשְׁכַת לַיְלָה.

13 וַיְהִי בַּחֲצִי הַלַּיְלָה:

King Belshazzar After Nebuchadnezzar exiled the Jews from Judah, in 586 B.C.E., he decided to integrate the best and the brightest of them into his court. Assigned a daily ration of royal food and wine, they were to be taught for three years, then some of them would serve his government. Among them were Daniel, Hananiah, Mishael, and Azariah.
The chief eunuch gave them Babylonian names: Belteshazzar, Shadrach, Meshach, and Abed-nego.
King Belshazzar, Nebuchadnezzar's son, gave a feast using the utensils plundered from the Temple in Jerusalem. During the drunken feast, a hand wrote the words *mene mene tekel upharsin* on the wall. Daniel interpreted them as meaning that Belshazzar would be overthrown by the Medes and Persians. That very night Belshazzar was killed, and Darius the Mede became king (Daniel 5:-16:11).

IT HAPPENED AT MIDNIGHT!

At night <u>the Assyrian armies</u> besieging Jerusalem were stricken.
 At night the idol Bel and its pedestal were overthrown in the dark.
At night, You revealed Your mysteries in a vision to Daniel.

IT HAPPENED AT MIDNIGHT!

At night <u>King Belshazzar,</u> of Babylon, who drank from the holy
vessels, was slain.
 At night Daniel, was saved from the lion's den.
At night Haman wrote his decrees of hate.

IT HAPPENED AT MIDNIGHT!

At night You achieved Your victory over Haman in the sleeplessness of
Ahasuerus.
You will squeeze the enemy as in a winepress for them that ask:
"Watchman, what of the night?"
Like the watchman, You will respond:
"The morning has come even as the night."

IT HAPPENED AT MIDNIGHT!

May the day come which is neither day nor night.
O Eternal, make known that You rule the day and also the night.
Appoint guards over Your city all day and all night.
Brighten the darkness of the night.

IT HAPPENED AT MIDNIGHT!

The Assyrian armies King Hezekiah of Judah (ca. 725-697 B.C.E.)
formed a secret alliance with Egypt and Babylonia, and refused to pay
tribute to Sargon, king of Assyria. When Sargon died, the allies decided
to revolt against Assyria. Sennacharib, Sargon's successor, learned of the
revolt and swiftly moved to crush it. The Assyrians besieged Jerusalem.
Guided by King Hezekiah and the prophet Isaiah, the city bravely
resisted.
Soon food became scarce and surrender became inevitable. Then, miraculously, "it happened at midnight." A plague struck the Assyrian camp and
thousands of enemy soldiers perished in the epidemic.
The prophet Isaiah mourned for the ravaged land of Judah. Yet, even
in the midst of ruined cities and towns, there were prayers of
thanksgiving, for Judah had miraculously survived the Assyrian onslaught.

On the second Seder night say:

וּבְכֵן וַאֲמַרְתֶּם זֶבַח פֶּסַח:

1 אֹמֶץ גְּבוּרוֹתֶיךָ הִפְלֵאתָ בַּפֶּסַח. בְּרֹאשׁ כָּל־מוֹעֲדוֹת נִשֵּׂאתָ פֶּסַח.

2 גִּלִּיתָ לְאֶזְרָחִי חֲצוֹת לֵיל־פֶּסַח. וַאֲמַרְתֶּם זֶבַח פֶּסַח:

3 דְּלָתָיו דָּפַקְתָּ כְּחֹם הַיּוֹם בַּפֶּסַח. הִסְעִיד נוֹצְצִים עֻגוֹת מַצּוֹת

4 בַּפֶּסַח. וְאֶל־הַבָּקָר רָץ זֵכֶר לְשׁוֹר עֵרֶךְ פֶּסַח. וַאֲמַרְתֶּם זֶבַח פֶּסַח:

5 זֹעֲמוּ סְדוֹמִים וְלוֹהֲטוּ בָּאֵשׁ בַּפֶּסַח. חֻלַּץ לוֹט מֵהֶם וּמַצּוֹת אָפָה

6 בְּקֵץ פֶּסַח. טִאטֵאתָ אַדְמַת מוֹף וְנוֹף בְּעָבְרְךָ בַּפֶּסַח.

7 וַאֲמַרְתֶּם זֶבַח פֶּסַח:

8 יָהּ, רֹאשׁ כָּל־אוֹן מָחַצְתָּ בְּלֵיל שִׁמּוּר פֶּסַח. כַּבִּיר עַל־בֵּן בְּכוֹר

9 פָּסַחְתָּ בְּדַם פֶּסַח. לְבִלְתִּי תֵּת מַשְׁחִית לָבֹא בִּפְתָחַי בַּפֶּסַח.

10 וַאֲמַרְתֶּם זֶבַח פֶּסַח:

11 מְסֻגֶּרֶת סֻגָּרָה בְּעִתּוֹתֵי פֶּסַח. נִשְׁמְדָה מִדְיָן בִּצְלִיל שְׂעוֹרֵי עֹמֶר

12 פֶּסַח. שֹׂרְפוּ מִשְׁמַנֵּי פּוּל וְלוּד בִּיקַד יְקוֹד פֶּסַח.

13 וַאֲמַרְתֶּם זֶבַח פֶּסַח:

14 עוֹד הַיּוֹם בְּנֹב לַעֲמֹד עַד גָּעָה עוֹנַת פֶּסַח. פַּס יָד כָּתְבָה לְקַעֲקֵעַ

15 צוּל בַּפֶּסַח. צָפֹה הַצָּפִית עָרוֹךְ הַשֻּׁלְחָן בַּפֶּסַח.

16 וַאֲמַרְתֶּם זֶבַח פֶּסַח:

17 קָהָל כִּנְּסָה הֲדַסָּה צוֹם לְשַׁלֵּשׁ בַּפֶּסַח. רֹאשׁ מִבֵּית רָשָׁע מָחַצְתָּ

18 בְּעֵץ חֲמִשִּׁים בַּפֶּסַח. שְׁתֵּי אֵלֶּה רֶגַע תָּבִיא לְעוּצִית בַּפֶּסַח. תָּעֹז

19 יָדְךָ וְתָרוּם יְמִינְךָ כְּלֵיל הִתְקַדֶּשׁ חַג פֶּסַח.

20 וַאֲמַרְתֶּם זֶבַח פֶּסַח:

Jericho Jericho was the first city attacked by the invading Israelites as they crossed the Jordan River into the Promised Land.
The strong gates of Jericho were closed, and the thick stone walls were manned by expert archers. So God said to Joshua, "You and your soldiers must walk around the city once a day for six days, followed by seven priests walking ahead of the Ark, each carrying a shofar. And on the seventh day you and your army must walk around the city seven times with the priests blowing their shofars. Then they are to give one giant blast and all the people are to give one mighty shout, and the walls of Jericho will come falling down."

continued on page 141

On the second Seder night say:
THIS IS THE PASSOVER OFFERING!

On Passover, You displayed your power.
Above all festivals You praised the Passover.
On Passover, You revealed Israel's destiny to Abraham.

THIS IS THE PASSOVER OFFERING!

On Passover, You knocked at his doors in the heat of the day.
On Passover, He served the angels cakes of unleavened bread.
For Passover, He ran to the herd to fetch an offering.

THIS IS THE PASSOVER OFFERING!

On Passover, the Sodomites provoked God and were consumed by fire.
On Passover, Lot separated from them and baked unleavened bread.
On Passover, You swept Egypt clean when You passed through it.

THIS IS THE PASSOVER OFFERING!

On Passover, You smote every Egyptian firstborn on the watch night.
On Passover, You passed over Israel's firstborn.
On Passover, You permitted no enemy to enter Israel's doors.

THIS IS THE PASSOVER OFFERING!

On Passover, the walls of Jericho fell.
On Passover, Midian was destroyed by a loaf of barley bread the size of omer.
On Passover, the Assyrians were burned in a mighty fire.

THIS IS THE PASSOVER OFFERING!

On Passover, Sennacherib met disaster at Zion's gate,
On Passover, the hand wrote on the wall in Babylon,
On Passover, the reveling city met its doom.

THIS IS THE PASSOVER OFFERING!

On Passover, Queen Esther assembled the Jews to fast for three days.
On Passover, Haman was hanged on the gallows fifty cubits high.
On Passover, You inflicted a double punishment on our enemies.
On Passover, your hands were uplifted.

THIS IS THE PASSOVER OFFERING!

On the seventh day, and on the seventh march around the city, as the priests blew a loud blast, the walls of Jericho came tumbling down and the city was conquered.

This is the Passover offering This song is an alphabetic acrostic listing the various miracles that occurred on the night of Passover. Eleazar El-Kalir is said to have written this song.

כִּי לוֹ נָאֶה. כִּי לוֹ יָאֶה:

אַדִּיר בִּמְלוּכָה. בָּחוּר כַּהֲלָכָה. גְּדוּדָיו יֹאמְרוּ לוֹ. לְךָ וּלְךָ.

לְךָ כִּי לְךָ. לְךָ אַף לְךָ. לְךָ יְיָ הַמַּמְלָכָה.

כִּי לוֹ נָאֶה. כִּי לוֹ יָאֶה:

דָּגוּל בִּמְלוּכָה. הָדוּר כַּהֲלָכָה. וָתִיקָיו יֹאמְרוּ לוֹ. לְךָ וּלְךָ.

לְךָ כִּי לְךָ. לְךָ אַף לְךָ. לְךָ יְיָ הַמַּמְלָכָה.

כִּי לוֹ נָאֶה. כִּי לוֹ יָאֶה:

זַכַּאי בִּמְלוּכָה. חָסִין כַּהֲלָכָה. טַפְסְרָיו יֹאמְרוּ לוֹ. לְךָ וּלְךָ.

לְךָ כִּי לְךָ. לְךָ אַף לְךָ. לְךָ יְיָ הַמַּמְלָכָה.

כִּי לוֹ נָאֶה. כִּי לוֹ יָאֶה:

יָחִיד בִּמְלוּכָה. כַּבִּיר כַּהֲלָכָה. לִמּוּדָיו יֹאמְרוּ לוֹ. לְךָ וּלְךָ.

לְךָ כִּי לְךָ. לְךָ אַף לְךָ. לְךָ יְיָ הַמַּמְלָכָה.

כִּי לוֹ נָאֶה. כִּי לוֹ יָאֶה:

מוֹשֵׁל בִּמְלוּכָה. נוֹרָא כַּהֲלָכָה. סְבִיבָיו יֹאמְרוּ לוֹ. לְךָ וּלְךָ.

לְךָ כִּי לְךָ. לְךָ אַף לְךָ. לְךָ יְיָ הַמַּמְלָכָה.

כִּי לוֹ נָאֶה. כִּי לוֹ יָאֶה:

עָנָיו בִּמְלוּכָה. פּוֹדֶה כַּהֲלָכָה. צַדִּיקָיו יֹאמְרוּ לוֹ. לְךָ וּלְךָ.

לְךָ כִּי לְךָ. לְךָ אַף לְךָ. לְךָ יְיָ הַמַּמְלָכָה.

כִּי לוֹ נָאֶה. כִּי לוֹ יָאֶה:

TO HIM IT IS FITTING, TO HIM IT IS DUE

Mighty in majesty, Supreme indeed!
God's legions sing:
To you, O God, belongs the world's sovereignty.

TO HIM IT IS FITTING, TO HIM IT IS DUE

First in majesty, Glorious indeed!
God's faithful sing:
To you, O God, is the world's sovereignty.

TO HIM IT IS FITTING, TO HIM IT IS DUE

Pure in majesty, Powerful indeed!
God's attendants sing to Him:
To You, O God, is the world's sovereignty.

TO HIM IT IS FITTING, TO HIM IT IS DUE

Matchless in majesty, Great indeed
God's disciples sing:
To You, O God, is the world's sovereignty.

TO HIM IT IS FITTING, TO HIM IT IS DUE

Ruling in majesty, Revered indeed!
His angels sing to Him:
To You, O God, is the world's sovereignty.

TO HIM IT IS FITTING, TO HIM IT IS DUE

Humble in majesty, Redeemer indeed!
God's righteous sing:
To You, O God, is the world's sovereignty.

1 קָדוֹשׁ בִּמְלוּכָה. רַחוּם כַּהֲלָכָה. שִׁנְאַנָּיו יֹאמְרוּ לוֹ. לְךָ וּלְךָ.

2 לְךָ כִּי לְךָ. לְךָ אַף לְךָ. לְךָ יְיָ הַמַּמְלָכָה.

3 **כִּי לוֹ נָאֶה. כִּי לוֹ יָאֶה:**

4 תַּקִּיף בִּמְלוּכָה. תּוֹמֵךְ כַּהֲלָכָה. תְּמִימָיו יֹאמְרוּ לוֹ. לְךָ וּלְךָ.

5 לְךָ כִּי לְךָ. לְךָ אַף לְךָ. לְךָ יְיָ הַמַּמְלָכָה.

6 **כִּי לוֹ נָאֶה. כִּי לוֹ יָאֶה:**

THE FOURTH CUP OF WINE
*All together, raise your cups and celebrate the
holy joy of freedom with the following blessing:*

7 בָּרוּךְ אַתָּה יְיָ אֱלֹהֵינוּ מֶלֶךְ הָעוֹלָם, בּוֹרֵא, פְּרִי הַגָּפֶן:

The fourth cup of wine You now recite the blessing and drink the
fourth cup of wine. This cup of wine recalls the Eternal's fourth
promise: "I choose you to be My people." Drink the fourth cup of wine.

TO HIM IT IS FITTING, TO HIM IT IS DUE
Holy in majesty, Merciful indeed!
His myriads sing to Him:
Yours alone, O God, is the world's sovereignty.

TO HIM IT IS FITTING, TO HIM IT IS DUE
Almighty in majesty, Sustainer indeed!
His upright sing to Him:
Yours alone, O God, is the world's sovereignty.
TO HIM IT IS FITTING, TO HIM IT IS DUE

THE FOURTH CUP OF WINE
*All together, raise your cups and celebrate the
holy joy of freedom with the following blessing:*

**Blessed are You, Eternal our God, Ruler of the universe,
Creator of <u>the fruit of the vine.</u>**

Baruch atah adonay elohey-nu melech ha-o-lam borey-p'ree ha-ga-fen.

The fruit of the vine A sage suggests that the four cups of wine represent
the four matriarchs, Sarah, Rebecca, Rachel, and Leah, for through the
merit of the matriarchs and patriarchs Israel was redeemed from Egypt.
It is customary to use red wine at the Seder, since it serves as a reminder
of the blood that was smeared on the doorposts of the Israelite homes in
Egypt. The blood was a sign of protection when God passed over the
Israelite homes, not permitting the death of the firstborn.
Using red wine is also a reminder of the Jewish children that Pharaoh
slaughtered. Even after 3,000 years we remember the tragedy. Today, using
red wine also reminds us of the millions of Jews who were murdered
during the Holocaust.

Drink the fourth cup of wine while reclining
On the Sabbath add the words in parenthesis.

1 **בָּרוּךְ אַתָּה** יְיָ אֱלֹהֵינוּ מֶלֶךְ הָעוֹלָם, עַל־הַגֶּפֶן וְעַל־

2 פְּרִי הַגֶּפֶן, וְעַל־תְּנוּבַת הַשָּׂדֶה, וְעַל־אֶרֶץ חֶמְדָּה טוֹבָה

3 וּרְחָבָה, שֶׁרָצִיתָ וְהִנְחַלְתָּ לַאֲבוֹתֵינוּ, לֶאֱכוֹל מִפִּרְיָהּ

4 וְלִשְׁבּוֹעַ מִטּוּבָהּ. רַחֶם נָא יְיָ אֱלֹהֵינוּ עַל־יִשְׂרָאֵל עַמֶּךָ,

5 וְעַל־יְרוּשָׁלַיִם עִירֶךָ, וְעַל־צִיּוֹן מִשְׁכַּן כְּבוֹדֶךָ, וְעַל־מִזְבְּחֶךָ

6 וְעַל־הֵיכָלֶךָ. וּבְנֵה יְרוּשָׁלַיִם עִיר הַקֹּדֶשׁ בִּמְהֵרָה בְיָמֵינוּ

7 וְהַעֲלֵנוּ לְתוֹכָהּ וְשַׂמְּחֵנוּ בְּבִנְיָנָהּ וְנֹאכַל מִפִּרְיָהּ, וְנִשְׂבַּע

8 מִטּוּבָהּ וּנְבָרֶכְךָ עָלֶיהָ בִּקְדֻשָּׁה וּבְטָהֳרָה:

9 (on Sabbath **וּרְצֵה וְהַחֲלִיצֵנוּ בְּיוֹם הַשַּׁבָּת הַזֶּה**) וְשַׂמְּחֵנוּ

10 בְּיוֹם חַג הַמַּצּוֹת הַזֶּה: כִּי אַתָּה יְיָ טוֹב וּמֵטִיב לַכֹּל וְנוֹדֶה־

11 לְּךָ עַל־הָאָרֶץ וְעַל־פְּרִי הַגֶּפֶן: בָּרוּךְ אַתָּה יְיָ, עַל־הָאָרֶץ

12 וְעַל־פְּרִי הַגֶּפֶן:

After eating other foods:

13 **בָּרוּךְ אַתָּה** יְיָ אֱלֹהֵינוּ מֶלֶךְ הָעוֹלָם, בּוֹרֵא נְפָשׁוֹת רַבּוֹת

14 וְחֶסְרוֹנָן, עַל כָּל מַה שֶּׁבָּרָא לְהַחֲיוֹת בָּהֶם נֶפֶשׁ כָּל חָי.

15 בָּרוּךְ חֵי הָעוֹלָמִים:

The home of Your glory In order to provide a place where the Israelites could worship God, Moses appointed two craftsmen, Bezalel and Oholiab, to construct a sanctuary. The sanctuary was designed to be portable. The primary structure was the Tent of Meeting, a large tent with a strong wooden frame. It consisted of an inner court and an outer court, separated by curtains. In the inner court stood the Tabernacle. This was divided by a curtain or veil into the Holy Place where the peiest would burn incense offerings on the altar.

The Torah describes the Ark of the Covenant in which the two holy tablets brought down by Moses were kept. The Ark was a portable shrine made of acacia wood, with handles for carrying it from place to place. Atop it were two carved angels called cherubim.

Drink the fourth cup of wine while reclining
On the Sabbath add the words in parenthesis.

Blessed are you, Eternal Ruler of the universe, for the vine and
for the fruit of the vine, for the produce of the field and for
the precious, good, and spacious land which You favored
and gave to our ancestors, to eat of its fruit, and to enjoy its
goodness, Have compassion, O Eternal our God, upon
Zion, the <u>home of Your glory,</u> and upon Your altar and Your
Temple. Rebuild Jerusalem, the holy city, speedily in our
days. Lead us there, and gladden us with its rebuilding:
may we eat of its fruit and enjoy its blessings;
and we will bless You for this in holiness and purity.

"Be gracious to us and strengthen us on this Sabbath day."Grant
us joy on <u>this festival of Passover,</u> for You. O God, are good
and beneficent to all; and we therefore give thanks unto You
for the land and the fruit of the vine. Blessed are You,
O Eternal, blessed are You, for the land and the fruit of the
vine.

After eating other foods:
Blessed are You, Eternal our God, Ruler of the universe,
Creator of all living beings. We thank You for all that You
have created to sustain us, Blessed be the Eternal.

This festival of Passover Passover is the most famous and festive of our
holidays. It begins on the eve of the 15th day of the Hebrew month of
Nisan and lasts for eight days. On Passover we remember how Moses
freed the Israelites who were slaves in Egypt. The holiday received its
name from the Hebrew word *pasach.* When all the firstborn sons of the
Egyptians were killed in the tenth plague, the Angel of Death passed over
(pasach) the homes of the Jews and their lives were saved. Passover is also
called the Feast of Matzot, because the Jews left Egypt in such a hurry
they did not have time to let the dough for bread rise. This bread was flat
and hard. The flat unleavened bread is called matzah.

CONCLUSION OF THE SEDER (14) נִרְצָה

1 חֲסַל סִדּוּר פֶּסַח כְּהִלְכָתוֹ.

2 כְּכָל מִשְׁפָּטוֹ וְחֻקָּתוֹ.

3 כַּאֲשֶׁר זָכִינוּ, לְסַדֵּר אוֹתוֹ,

4 כֵּן נִזְכֶּה לַעֲשׂוֹתוֹ:

5 זָךְ שׁוֹכֵן מְעוֹנָה.

6 קוֹמֵם קְהַל עֲדַת מִי מָנָה.

7 בְּקָרוֹב נַהֵל, נִטְעֵי כַנָּה

8 פְּדוּיִים לְצִיּוֹן בְּרִנָּה:

All Sing

9 לְשָׁנָה הַבָּאָה בִּירוּשָׁלָיִם: *L'shanah HaBa'ah B'yerushalayim*

Next Year In Jerusalem In this politically unstable time, we pray for the future of the State of Israel and its people.
1. "Next Year in Jerusalem" refers to peace in Jerusalem.
2. "Redeemed people" refers to peace in Israel externally with their Arab neighbors, and internally among the various religious and ethnic groups.

THE COUNTING OF THE OMER
On the second night of Pesach we begin to count the Omer, leading to Shavuot.

10 בָּרוּךְ אַתָּה יְיָ אֱלֹהֵינוּ מֶלֶךְ הָעוֹלָם. אֲשֶׁר קִדְּשָׁנוּ בְּמִצְוֹתָיו

11 וְצִוָּנוּ עַל סְפִירַת הָעוֹמֶר:

12 הַיּוֹם יוֹם אֶחָד לָעוֹמֶר:

Omer Jewish mystics believe that each of the seven weeks of counting the Omer is associated with one of the seven Sefirot that describe the qualities of God: Chesed, love, Gevurah, power, Tiferet, beauty, Netzach, glory, Hod, glory, Yesod, foundation, Shechinah, sovereignty.

Omer In Temple times, on the second day of Passover, the priest would measure out an omer of grain as an offering to God to protect the farmer and his crops. Starting from this day the people would count the days between the Omer grain offering and Shavuot. Today, we call the seven weeks (49 days) the time of the Counting of the Omer. *continued on page 149*

NIRTZAH - CONCLUSION OF THE SEDER (14)
The Passover Seder is ended.

According to custom and law.

As we were worthy to celebrate it this year,

So may we perform it in future years.

O Pure One in heaven above,

Speedily lead Your <u>redeemed people</u>

To Zion in joy.

NEXT YEAR IN JERUSALEM
All Sing
L'shanah HaBaah B'yerushalyim

Next year in Jerusalem. We end the Seder with the Hebrew words
L'shanah haba'ah b'yerushalayim, "Next year in Jerusalem." Our people
began in the land of Israel thousands of years ago. Our people loved the
land of Israel. They used to say that Israel was the center of the world.
And right in the middle of Israel were Jerusalem and the Holy Temple.
But almost 2,000 years ago, most of the Jews were driven out of Israel.
Then in 1948, after much fighting, the State of Israel was set up again.
Once again Israel is free. Once again the holy city of Jerusalem is the
capital of Israel.

THE COUNTING OF THE OMER
On the second night of Pesach we begin to count the Omer,
leading to Shavuot.

**Blessed are You, Eternal our God, Ruler of the universe, who
has made us holy with commandments and commanded us to
count the <u>Omer.</u>**

Today is the first day of the Omer:

**May the Merciful One restore the Temple service to its rightful place
for us, speedily in our days, Amen.**

Omer This is a solemn time and some people do not schedule
celebrations or hold weddings. The counting continues for 49 days
leading up to Shavuot, the festival of the giving of the Ten
Commandments.

1   **אַדִּיר הוּא.** יִבְנֶה בֵיתוֹ בְּקָרוֹב. בִּמְהֵרָה בִּמְהֵרָה, בְּיָמֵינוּ

2   בְּקָרוֹב. אֵל בְּנֵה. אֵל בְּנֵה. **בְּנֵה בֵיתְךָ בְּקָרוֹב:**

3   **בָּחוּר הוּא. גָּדוֹל הוּא. דָּגוּל הוּא.** יִבְנֶה בֵיתוֹ בְּקָרוֹב.

4   בִּמְהֵרָה בִּמְהֵרָה, בְּיָמֵינוּ בְּקָרוֹב. אֵל בְּנֵה. אֵל בְּנֵה. **בְּנֵה**

5   **בֵיתְךָ בְּקָרוֹב:**

6   **הָדוּר הוּא. וָתִיק הוּא. זַכַּאי הוּא. חָסִיד הוּא.** יִבְנֶה בֵיתוֹ

7   בְּקָרוֹב. בִּמְהֵרָה בִּמְהֵרָה, בְּיָמֵינוּ בְּקָרוֹב. אֵל בְּנֵה. אֵל

8   בְּנֵה. **בְּנֵה בֵיתְךָ בְּקָרוֹב:**

9   **טָהוֹר הוּא. יָחִיד הוּא. כַּבִּיר הוּא. לָמוּד הוּא. מֶלֶךְ הוּא.**

10   **נוֹרָא הוּא. סַגִּיב הוּא. עִזּוּז הוּא. פּוֹדֶה הוּא. צַדִּיק הוּא.**

11   יִבְנֶה בֵיתוֹ בְּקָרוֹב. בִּמְהֵרָה בִּמְהֵרָה, בְּיָמֵינוּ בְּקָרוֹב. אֵל

12   בְּנֵה. אֵל בְּנֵה. **בְּנֵה בֵיתְךָ בְּקָרוֹב:**

13   **קָדוֹשׁ הוּא. רַחוּם הוּא. שַׁדַּי הוּא. תַּקִּיף הוּא.** יִבְנֶה בֵיתוֹ

14   בְּקָרוֹב. בִּמְהֵרָה בִּמְהֵרָה, בְּיָמֵינוּ בְּקָרוֹב. אֵל בְּנֵה. אֵל

15   בְּנֵה. **בְּנֵה בֵיתְךָ בְּקָרוֹב:**

The Eternal is mighty Adir Hu is an alphabetical acrostic prayer for the rebuilding of the Temple. The author is unknown. It was added to the Haggadah in 15th-century Germany.

ADIR HU

The Eternal is mighty!
  May the Temple be rebuilt.
Speedily, speedily,
  In our lifetime, soon.

O Eternal, rebuild, O Eternal, rebuild,
  Rebuild Your Temple soon.

The Eternal is first, great and renowned!
  Rebuild Your Temple soon.

Speedily, speedily,
  In our lifetime soon.

O Eternal, rebuild, O Eternal, rebuild,
  Rebuild Your Temple soon.

Speedily, speedily,
  In our lifetime soon.

O Eternal, rebuild, O God, rebuild,
  Rebuild Your Temple soon.

The Eternal is pure, mighty, wise and majestic,
Holy, strong, redeemer and rightous!
  Rebuild your Temple soon.

Speedily, speedily,
  in our lifetime soon.

O Eternal, rebuild, O Eternal, rebuild
  Rebuild Your Temple soon.

The Eternal is holy, merciful, powerful and almighty!
  Rebuild Your Temple soon.

The Eternal is holy, merciful, powerful and almighty!
  Rebuild Your Temple soon.

Speedily, speedily
In our lifetime soon.
O Eternal, rebuild, O Eternal, rebuild Your Temple soon.
O Lord, speedily,
Rebuild Jerusalem.
Blessed are You, O Eternal, our God,
Who will rebuild Jerusalem.

ECHAD MI YODE'A

1 אֶחָד מִי יוֹדֵעַ? אֶחָד אֲנִי יוֹדֵעַ. אֶחָד אֱלֹהֵינוּ שֶׁבַּשָּׁמַיִם
2 וּבָאָרֶץ:

3 שְׁנַיִם מִי יוֹדֵעַ? שְׁנַיִם אֲנִי יוֹדֵעַ. שְׁנֵי לֻחוֹת הַבְּרִית. אֶחָד
4 אֱלֹהֵינוּ שֶׁבַּשָּׁמַיִם וּבָאָרֶץ:

5 שְׁלֹשָׁה מִי יוֹדֵעַ? שְׁלֹשָׁה אֲנִי יוֹדֵעַ. שְׁלֹשָׁה אָבוֹת. שְׁנֵי
6 לֻחוֹת הַבְּרִית. אֶחָד אֱלֹהֵינוּ שֶׁבַּשָּׁמַיִם וּבָאָרֶץ:

7 אַרְבַּע מִי יוֹדֵעַ? אַרְבַּע אֲנִי יוֹדֵעַ. אַרְבַּע אִמָּהוֹת. שְׁלֹשָׁה
8 אָבוֹת. שְׁנֵי לֻחוֹת הַבְּרִית. אֶחָד אֱלֹהֵינוּ שֶׁבַּשָּׁמַיִם וּבָאָרֶץ:

9 חֲמִשָּׁה מִי יוֹדֵעַ? חֲמִשָּׁה אֲנִי יוֹדֵעַ. חֲמִשָּׁה חוּמְשֵׁי תוֹרָה.
10 אַרְבַּע אִמָּהוֹת. שְׁלֹשָׁה אָבוֹת. שְׁנֵי לֻחוֹת הַבְּרִית. אֶחָד
11 אֱלֹהֵינוּ שֶׁבַּשָּׁמַיִם וּבָאָרֶץ:

Who knows one? Echad Mi Yode'a is a riddle song as well as a short
course in Jewish history and customs. Who knows one, who knows two,
who knows three? Do you know the answers?

I know three The three Fathers are Abraham, Isaac, and Jacob.

I know four The four Mothers are Sarah, Rebecca, Leah, and Rachel.

WHO KNOWS ONE?

<u>Who knows one?</u> I know one.
>One is our God, in heaven and on earth.

Who knows two? I know two.
>Two are the Tablets of the Covenant;
>One is our God, in heaven and on earth.

Who knows three? <u>I know three.</u>
>Three are the Fathers;
>Two are the Tablets of the Covenant;
>One is our God, in heaven and on earth.

Who knows four? <u>I know four.</u>
>Four are the Mothers;
>Three are the Fathers;
>Two are the Tablets of the Covenant;
>One is our God, in heaven and on earth.

Who knows five? <u>I know five.</u>
>Five are the books of the Torah;
>Four are the Mothers;
>Three are the Fathers;
>Two are the Tablets of the Covenant;
>One is our God, in heaven and on earth.

I know five The Torah which Moses received on Mount Sinai is also called the Five Books of Moses. The Five Books are: Genesis, Exodus, Leviticus, Numbers, and Deuteronomy. The story of Passover is found in the Book of Exodus.

The complete Hebrew Bible is called the TaNaK. It consist of three divisions; Torah (Five Books of Moses), Nevi'im (Prophets), and Ketuvim (Writings). The name TaNaK comes from the first letters of each of the three divisions. *T* is for Torah, *N* is for Nevi'im, and *K* is for Ketuvim.

1 **שִׁשָּׁה מִי יוֹדֵעַ? שִׁשָּׁה אֲנִי יוֹדֵעַ.** שִׁשָּׁה סִדְרֵי מִשְׁנָה. חֲמִשָּׁה

2 חוּמְשֵׁי תוֹרָה. אַרְבַּע אִמָּהוֹת. שְׁלֹשָׁה אָבוֹת. שְׁנֵי לֻחוֹת

3 הַבְּרִית. אֶחָד אֱלֹהֵינוּ שֶׁבַּשָּׁמַיִם וּבָאָרֶץ:

4 **שִׁבְעָה מִי יוֹדֵעַ? שִׁבְעָה אֲנִי יוֹדֵעַ.** שִׁבְעָה יְמֵי שַׁבַּתָּא.

5 שִׁשָּׁה סִדְרֵי מִשְׁנָה. חֲמִשָּׁה חוּמְשֵׁי תוֹרָה. אַרְבַּע אִמָּהוֹת.

6 שְׁלֹשָׁה אָבוֹת. שְׁנֵי לֻחוֹת הַבְּרִית. אֶחָד אֱלֹהֵינוּ שֶׁבַּשָּׁמַיִם

7 וּבָאָרֶץ:

8 **שְׁמוֹנָה מִי יוֹדֵעַ? שְׁמוֹנָה אֲנִי יוֹדֵעַ.** שְׁמוֹנָה יְמֵי מִילָה.

9 שִׁבְעָה יְמֵי שַׁבַּתָּא. שִׁשָּׁה סִדְרֵי מִשְׁנָה. חֲמִשָּׁה חוּמְשֵׁי

10 תוֹרָה. אַרְבַּע אִמָּהוֹת. שְׁלֹשָׁה אָבוֹת. שְׁנֵי לֻחוֹת הַבְּרִית.

11 אֶחָד אֱלֹהֵינוּ שֶׁבַּשָּׁמַיִם וּבָאָרֶץ:

12 **תִּשְׁעָה מִי יוֹדֵעַ? תִּשְׁעָה אֲנִי יוֹדֵעַ.** תִּשְׁעָה יַרְחֵי לֵדָה.

13 שְׁמוֹנָה יְמֵי מִילָה. שִׁבְעָה יְמֵי שַׁבַּתָּא. שִׁשָּׁה סִדְרֵי מִשְׁנָה.

14 חֲמִשָּׁה חוּמְשֵׁי תוֹרָה. אַרְבַּע אִמָּהוֹת. שְׁלֹשָׁה אָבוֹת. שְׁנֵי

15 לֻחוֹת הַבְּרִית. אֶחָד אֱלֹהֵינוּ שֶׁבַּשָּׁמַיִם וּבָאָרֶץ:

The Mishnah The Oral Law is a commentary on the Torah explaining how the commandments are to be implemented. In time the Oral Law grew to such a huge size that very few could remember it. Around 200 B.C.E., Judah HaNasi and the scholars known as tannaim arranged and edited the commentaries and the legal decisions of the Oral Law into the Mishnah. It has six main divisions: Zeraim, seeds, Mo'ed, festivals. Mo'ed, festivals, Nashim, women, Nezikin, damages, Kadoshim, holy matters, and Taharot, purities, Later on scholars called amoraim collected the discussions and legal decisions since the completion of the Mishnah. These discussions and decisions are called the Gemara. Together the Mishnah and the Gemara make up the Talmud.

Who knows six? I know six.
> Six are the orders of the <u>Mishnah</u>;
> Five are the books of the Torah;
> Four are the Mothers;
> Three are the Fathers;
> Two are the Tablets of the Covenant;
> One is our God, in heaven and on earth.

Who knows seven? I know seven.
> Seven are the days of the week;
> Six are the orders of the Mishnah;
> Five are the books of the Torah;
> Four are the Mothers;
> Three are the Fathers;
> Two are the Tablets of the Covenant;
> One is our God, in heaven and on earth.

Who knows eight? I know eight.
> Eight are the days to circumcision;
> Seven are the days of the week;
> Six are the orders of the Mishnah;
> Five are the books of the Torah;
> Four are the Mothers;
> Three are the Fathers;
> Two are the Tablets of the Covenant;
> One is our God, in heaven and on earth.

Who knows nine? I know nine.
> Nine are the months to childbirth;
> Eight are the days to circumcision;
> Seven are the days of the week;
> Six are the orders of the Mishnah;
> Five are the books of the Torah;
> Four are the Mothers;
> Three are the Fathers;
> Two are the Tablets of the Covenant;
> One is our God, in heaven and on earth.

1 **עֲשָׂרָה מִי יוֹדֵעַ? עֲשָׂרָה אֲנִי יוֹדֵעַ.** עֲשָׂרָה דִבְּרַיָּא. תִּשְׁעָה

2 יַרְחֵי לֵדָה. שְׁמוֹנָה יְמֵי מִילָה. שִׁבְעָה יְמֵי שַׁבַּתָּא. שִׁשָּׁה

3 סִדְרֵי מִשְׁנָה, חֲמִשָּׁה חוּמְשֵׁי תוֹרָה. אַרְבַּע אִמָּהוֹת.

4 שְׁלֹשָׁה אָבוֹת. שְׁנֵי לֻחוֹת הַבְּרִית. אֶחָד אֱלֹהֵינוּ שֶׁבַּשָּׁמַיִם

5 וּבָאָרֶץ:

6 **אַחַד עָשָׂר מִי יוֹדֵעַ? אַחַד עָשָׂר אֲנִי יוֹדֵעַ.** אַחַד עָשָׂר

7 כּוֹכְבַיָּא. עֲשָׂרָה דִבְּרַיָּא. תִּשְׁעָה יַרְחֵי לֵדָה. שְׁמוֹנָה יְמֵי

8 מִילָה. שִׁבְעָה יְמֵי שַׁבַּתָּא. שִׁשָּׁה סִדְרֵי מִשְׁנָה, חֲמִשָּׁה

9 חוּמְשֵׁי תוֹרָה. אַרְבַּע אִמָּהוֹת. שְׁלֹשָׁה אָבוֹת. שְׁנֵי לֻחוֹת

10 הַבְּרִית. אֶחָד אֱלֹהֵינוּ שֶׁבַּשָּׁמַיִם וּבָאָרֶץ:

I know ten Right after Moses led the Children of Israel out of Egypt, he heard the voice of God telling him to go to the top of Mount Sinai. Moses stayed on the mountaintop for 40 days and 40 nights.
When he came back down to the people, he brought with him two stone tablets. Written on the tablets were the ten great laws which God had given him. These were the Ten Commandments, the most famous laws in the history of civilization. If the whole world lived up to these great laws, everyone would be happy and there would always be peace.

continued on page 157

Who knows ten? <u>I know ten.</u>

> Ten are the commandments;
> Nine are the months to childbirth;
> Eight are the days to circumcision;
> Seven are the days of the week;
> Six are the orders of the Mishnah;
> Five are the books of the Torah;
> Four are the Mothers;
> Three are the Fathers;
> Two are the Tablets of the Covenant;
> One is our God, in heaven and on earth.

Who knows eleven? I know eleven.

> Eleven are the stars in Joseph's dream.
> Ten are the commandments;
> Nine are the months to childbirth;
> Eight are the days to circumcision;
> Seven are the days of the week;
> Six are the orders of the Mishnah;
> Five are the books of the Torah;
> Four are the Mothers;
> Three are the Fathers;
> Two are the Tablets of the Covenant;
> One is our God, in heaven and on earth.

---

1. I am the Lord your God, who brought you out of the land of Egypt and liberated you from slavery.
2. You shall worship no other gods but Me.
3. You shall make no idols.
4. Remember the Sabbath day and keep it holy.
5. Honor your father and your mother.
6. You shall not kill.
7. You shall not commit adultery.
8. You shall not steal.
9. You shall not give false testimony.
10. You shall not be envious.

1 שְׁנֵים עָשָׂר מִי יוֹדֵעַ? שְׁנֵים עָשָׂר אֲנִי יוֹדֵעַ. שְׁנֵים עָשָׂר

2 שִׁבְטַיָּא. אַחַד עָשָׂר כּוֹכְבַיָּא. עֲשָׂרָה דִּבְּרַיָּא. תִּשְׁעָה יַרְחֵי

3 לֵדָה. שְׁמוֹנָה יְמֵי מִילָה. שִׁבְעָה יְמֵי שַׁבַּתָּא. שִׁשָּׁה סִדְרֵי

4 מִשְׁנָה. חֲמִשָּׁה חוּמְשֵׁי תוֹרָה. אַרְבַּע אִמָּהוֹת. שְׁלשָׁה

5 אָבוֹת. שְׁנֵי לֻחוֹת הַבְּרִית. אֶחָד אֱלֹהֵינוּ שֶׁבַּשָּׁמַיִם וּבָאָרֶץ:

6 שְׁלשָׁה עָשָׂר מִי יוֹדֵעַ? שְׁלשָׁה עָשָׂר אֲנִי יוֹדֵעַ. שְׁלשָׁה עָשָׂר

7 מִדַּיָּא. שְׁנֵים עָשָׂר שִׁבְטַיָּא. אַחַד עָשָׂר כּוֹכְבַיָּא. עֲשָׂרָה

8 דִּבְּרַיָּא. תִּשְׁעָה יַרְחֵי לֵדָה. שְׁמוֹנָה יְמֵי מִילָה. שִׁבְעָה יְמֵי

9 שַׁבַּתָּא. שִׁשָּׁה סִדְרֵי מִשְׁנָה. חֲמִשָּׁה חוּמְשֵׁי תוֹרָה. אַרְבַּע

10 אִמָּהוֹת. שְׁלשָׁה אָבוֹת. שְׁנֵי לֻחוֹת הַבְּרִית. אֶחָד אֱלֹהֵינוּ

11 שֶׁבַּשָּׁמַיִם וּבָאָרֶץ:

I know twelve Jacob had 12 sons, and their descendants became the 12 tribe of Israel. When the Israelites reached the shore of the Sea of Reeds, Adonai miraculously provided 12 pathways in the middle of the sea: one for each of the tribes.

Who knows twelve, <u>I know twelve.</u>

Twelve are the tribes of Israel;
Eleven are the stars in Joseph's dream;
Ten are the commandments;
Nine are the months to childbirth;
Eight are the days to circumcision;
Seven are the days of the week;
Six are the orders of the Mishnah;
Five are the books of the Torah;
Four are the Mothers;
Three are the Fathers;
Two are the Tablets of the Covenant;
One is our God, in heaven and on earth.

Who knows thirteen? I know thirteen.

Thirteen are God's attributes;
Twelve are the tribes of Israel;
Eleven are the stars in Joseph's dream;
Ten are the commandments;
Nine are the months to childbirth;
Eight are the days to circumcision;
Seven are the days of the week;
Six are the orders of the Mishnah;
Five are the books of the Torah;
Four are the Mothers;
Three are the Fathers;
Two are the Tablets of the Covenant;
One is our God, in heaven and on earth.

I know twelve The 12 tribes of Israel are:

Reuben	Issachar	Dan	Judah	Asher
Shimon	Zebulun	Naftali	Joseph (Ephraim and Manasseh)	
Levi	Benjamin	Gad		

CHAD GADYA

חַד גַּדְיָא. חַד גַּדְיָא. דְּזַבִּין אַבָּא בִּתְרֵי זוּזֵי. חַד גַּדְיָא. חַד 1
גַּדְיָא: 2

וְאָתָא שׁוּנְרָא. וְאָכְלָה לְגַדְיָא. דְּזַבִּין אַבָּא בִּתְרֵי זוּזֵי. חַד 3
גַּדְיָא. חַד גַּדְיָא: 4

וְאָתָא כַלְבָּא. וְנָשַׁךְ לְשׁוּנְרָא. דְּאָכְלָה לְגַדְיָא. דְּזַבִּין אַבָּא 5
בִּתְרֵי זוּזֵי. חַד גַּדְיָא. חַד גַּדְיָא: 6

וְאָתָא חוּטְרָא. וְהִכָּה לְכַלְבָּא דְּנָשַׁךְ לְשׁוּנְרָא. דְּאָכְלָה 7
לְגַדְיָא. דְּזַבִּין אַבָּא בִּתְרֵי זוּזֵי. חַד גַּדְיָא. חַד גַּדְיָא: 8

וְאָתָא נוּרָא. וְשָׂרַף לְחוּטְרָא. דְּהִכָּה לְכַלְבָּא דְּנָשַׁךְ 9
לְשׁוּנְרָא. דְּאָכְלָה לְגַדְיָא. דְּזַבִּין אַבָּא בִּתְרֵי זוּזֵי. חַד גַּדְיָא. 10
חַד גַּדְיָא: 11

וְאָתָא מַיָּא. וְכָבָה לְנוּרָא. דְּשָׂרַף לְחוּטְרָא. דְּהִכָּה לְכַלְבָּא. 12
דְּנָשַׁךְ לְשׁוּנְרָא. דְּאָכְלָה לְגַדְיָא. דְּזַבִּין אַבָּא בִּתְרֵי זוּזֵי. 13
חַד גַּדְיָא. חַד גַּדְיָא: 14

Chad Gadya - One Little Goat This rhythmic folksong describes the unhappy adventures of a little goat that was purchased for two zuzim (coins) by kind parents for their child.
In this parable we read the story of the Jewish people. Each and every time, a new power rises by force of arms.

ONE LITTLE GOAT

One little goat, one little goat.
  Chad Gadya, Chad Gadya.

That my parents bought for two zuzim,
One little goat, one little goat.

  Chad Gadya, Chad Gadya.
Then came a cat
That ate the goat
That my parents bought for two zuzim.
One little goat, one little goat.
  Chad Gadya, Chad Gadya.

Then came a dog and bit the cat
That ate the goat
That my parents bought for two zuzim.
One little goat, one little goat.
  Chad Gadya, Chad Gadya.

Then came a stick and beat the dog
That bit the cat that ate the goat
That my parents bought for two zuzim.
One little goat, one little goat.
  Chad Gadya, Chad Gadya

Then came fire and burned the stick
That beat the dog that bit the cat
That ate the goat
That my parents bought for two zuzim.
One little goat, one little goat.
  Chad Gadya, Chad Gadya

Then came water and quenched the fire
That burned the stick that beat the dog
That bit the cat that ate the goat
That my parents bought for two zuzim.
One little goat, one little goat.
  Chad Gadya, Chad Gadya

One little goat Some believe that Chad Gadya has a deeper meaning.
The little goat is the Jewish people, surrounded by enemies who end up
devouring each other. In the end justice triumphs and God destroys them
all.

1 וְאָתָא תוֹרָא. וְשָׁתָה לְמַיָּא. דְּכָבָה לְנוּרָא. דְּשָׂרַף לְחוּטְרָא.

2 דְּהִכָּה לְכַלְבָּא. דְּנָשַׁךְ לְשׁוּנְרָא. דְּאָכְלָה לְגַדְיָא. דְּזַבִּין

3 אַבָּא בִּתְרֵי זוּזֵי. חַד גַּדְיָא. חַד גַּדְיָא:

4 וְאָתָא הַשּׁוֹחֵט. וְשָׁחַט לְתוֹרָא. דְּשָׁתָה לְמַיָּא. דְּכָבָה

5 לְנוּרָא. דְּשָׂרַף לְחוּטְרָא. דְּהִכָּה לְכַלְבָּא. דְּנָשַׁךְ לְשׁוּנְרָא.

6 דְּאָכְלָה לְגַדְיָא. דְּזַבִּין אַבָּא בִּתְרֵי זוּזֵי. חַד גַּדְיָא. חַד גַּדְיָא:

7 וְאָתָא מַלְאַךְ הַמָּוֶת. וְשָׁחַט לְשׁוֹחֵט דְּשָׁחַט לְתוֹרָא.

8 דְּשָׁתָה לְמַיָּא. דְּכָבָה לְנוּרָא. דְּשָׂרַף לְחוּטְרָא. דְּהִכָּה

9 לְכַלְבָּא. דְּנָשַׁךְ לְשׁוּנְרָא. דְּאָכְלָה לְגַדְיָא. דְּזַבִּין אַבָּא

10 בִּתְרֵי זוּזֵי. חַד גַּדְיָא. חַד גַּדְיָא:

11 וְאָתָא הַקָּדוֹשׁ בָּרוּךְ הוּא. וְשָׁחַט לְמַלְאַךְ הַמָּוֶת. דְּשָׁחַט

12 לְשׁוֹחֵט. דְּשָׁחַט לְתוֹרָא. דְּשָׁתָה לְמַיָּא. דְּכָבָה לְנוּרָא,

13 דְּשָׂרַף לְחוּטְרָא. דְּהִכָּה לְכַלְבָּא. דְּנָשַׁךְ לְשׁוּנְרָא. דְּאָכְלָה

14 לְגַדְיָא. דְּזַבִּין אַבָּא בִּתְרֵי זוּזֵי. חַד גַּדְיָא. חַד גַּדְיָא:

Then came the shochet and slaughtered the ox
That drank the water that quenched the fire
That burned the stick that beat the dog
That bit the cat that ate the goat
That my parents bought for two zuzim.
One little goat, one little goat.
  Chad Gadya, Chad Gadya.

Then came the Angel of Death and killed the shochet
That slaughtered the ox
That drank the water that quenched the fire
That burned the stick that beat the dog
That bit the cat that ate the goat
That my parents bouught for two zuzim.
One little goat, one little goat.
  Chad Gadya, Chad Gadya

Then came the Holy One, blessed be He,
 And slew the Angel of Death
That killed the shochet that slaughtered the ox
That drank the water that quenched the fire
That burned the stick that beat the dog
That bit the cat that ate the goat
That my parents bought for two zuzim.
One little goat, one little goat.
  Chad Gadya, Chad Gadya

THE SEDER BLITZ

The passage of time dims the cells of memory. Yet there are special events that retain freshness and are not affected by the ticktock of the clock. During World War II, some 60 years ago, I was stationed in England, close to London. Hungry for the warmth of a Jewish family and a Shabbat meal, I found a kosher butcher shop in the East End of London and asked the butcher in Yiddish where I could find a kosher restaurant. A woman overheard me, and invited me for a Friday night meal. Her husband was fighting in North Africa and she was caring for two children, her mother, and an older sister. That night I climbed to the sixth floor of an old walkup. At the meal I recited the Kiddush and all the family, including myself, were teary eyed.

I especially remember the second night of Passover in 1944. The Nazi air force was pounding London with night bombers and V1 and V2 rockets. A special target was the East End of London, the so-called Jewish ghetto. Rachel invited me to conduct the Seder, and I managed to get a pass for the second night of Passover. We were all seated around the Seder table: Rachel, two children, her sister Leah, and the old infirm grandmother. As soon as one of the children asked "Why is this night different?" the air raid siren sounded. We immediately closed all the curtains. Shaken, I said, "Let's go down to the air raid shelter." Rachel and Leah insisted that we stay and continue the Seder. The bombardment lasted for about an hour, during which the building continually shook.

After the all-clear, I asked Rachel, "Why didn't we go down to the shelter?" Her direct, matter-of-fact reply was, "Grandma cannot make it down the six floors, and if God wills, we will go as one family."

The next morning I returned to see how the family was doing. As I reached their street, I saw a mass of destruction with rescue workers removing wounded and dead bodies. All of the structures around Rachel's building had been gutted by fire or hit by bombs. In the midst of the devastation, the only building left standing was Rachel's.

Time dulls the senses, but there are moments when I can still see the fires and feel the thud of bombs and see faces at the Seder table. That night was different, we all survived.

FROM THE MIDRASH

BIRTH OF MOSES

"A son will be born to my mother and father who will deliver Israel from Egypt." Our wise men tell us that this was the prophecy made by Miriam, sister of Moses.

When Moses was born, his tiny face shone with a bright, heavenly light. Then his parents knew that what Miriam had prophesied would come to pass.

The prophecy was fulfilled when, many years later, Moses led the Children of Israel out of Egypt to the Promised Land.

THE EGYPTIAN PRINCESS

The daughter of the Pharaoh went to bathe in the river Nile with her servants. There, hidden in the bushes, they found the baby Moses in a basket.

The princess took the baby to the palace and raised him as her own son.

Why did the Princess and her maidens go bathing on that particular day? Our wise men tell us it was because God made that day as scorching hot as a furnace. The Lord wanted Moses to be found so that he could grow up to be a great leader for his people.

THE RED SEA

When the Children of Israel reached the Red Sea, God said to Moses: "Lift your rod above the sea. I will send a great wind to part the waters and make a dry path for My people."

Moses could have led the Israelites around the Red Sea. Then why did God command him to lead them across it?

Our wise men tell us that God wanted to punish the Egyptians and prove to them that the Lord's power was greater than any power on earth

And so the Israelites crossed the Red Sea safely, while the wicked Egyptian soldiers following them were drowned.

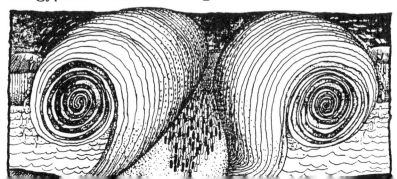

MOSES THE STUTTERER

Moses was a beautiful child. The princess loved baby Moses very much. She would spend her days playing with the baby.

The Pharaoh was also very fond of baby Moses. He would hold the baby on his lap and allow Moses to take the shiny golden crown from his head and play with it.

The Egyptian priests warned Pharaoh that this was a sign that someday Moses would take the Kingdom of Egypt away from him. The priests were so sure that they even suggested killing the baby. Pharaoh and his daughter refused to listen to their advice.

Finally, Pharaoh agreed to test the child. The priests placed a plate with a golden bar and a hot coal in front of baby Moses. If he picked up the gold, it would mean that he understood exactly what he was doing, and then he would be killed.

If the baby chose the hot coal, that would mean that he did not know what he was doing, and then he would remain alive.

The plate was placed before Moses. He reached for the shiny gold bar, but an angel moved his hand to the hot coal.

Moses picked up the burning coal and placed it on his lips. His tongue was burned and he became a stutterer. Moses' life was saved, and later on he freed his people from Egyptian slavery.

THE PI

MW01113796

Our wise men tell us that the Pharaoh of Egypt in... ...
palace, guarded by wild and ferocious beasts. When people tried to enter the palace gates, these beasts leaped at them and drove them away in terror.

One day, two men came to the palace gates. One was Aaron, brother of Moses, and the other was Moses himself. They came to ask the Pharaoh to free the Hebrews from slavery.

Moses and Aaron walked bravely up to the gates where the fierce beasts roared. Lo and behold! The animals became as tame as kittens. They licked Aaron's and Moses' hands, and the two Hebrew leaders walked through the gates unharmed.

THE TAMBOURINES

When Moses led the Hebrews out of Egypt, the people left in such a hurry that they did not even have time to bake their bread. They quickly gathered up the unleavened dough and fled.

Our wise men tell us that in spite of their great hurry, there was one thing they remembered to take. Every Hebrew woman brought along her tambourine.

So great was their faith that God would save them that they wanted to have their tambourines with them to celebrate their freedom with joyful singing and music.